HMH | (into) **Literature**™

Program Guide

Surviving & Thriving

IN THE CLASSROOM

GRADES 9-10

Printed in the U.S.A.

ISBN 978-0-358-43695-9

1 2 3 4 5 6 7 8 9 10   0607   29 28 27 26 25 24 23 22 21 20

4500817009

r10.20

Connected Teaching for ELA Educators

Dear Educators,

At HMH, **we have been listening** to your needs. Lean on us to help you

- connect students to the right **instruction**
- deliver flexible and innovative learning experiences built on the foundations of **best teaching practices** and **educational research**
- **bridge the digital divide** with instruction available in both print and digital formats, accessible online and offline
- provide a **reliable and valid growth measure** that monitors progress and achievement
- implement traditional classroom teaching and the tools to deliver instruction through **remote learning**
- foster students' **social and emotional growth** and build resilience through embedded SEL support
- teach with continuous, connected **professional learning** . . . and *do what you do best*

Flexible instruction for in-classroom and remote learning

Engaging teacher and student experience

Assessment and insights

Continuous connected professional learning

Personalized and adaptive supplemental solutions

Take a Look!

This Program Guide is your **professional companion** to help you to learn about your new program, *HMH Into Literature.*

Let's go!

Table of Contents

Introduction

4   **ELA Educators, We're Listening**

8   **Introducing *HMH Into Literature***

Program Tour

10   **Program at a Glance**

24   **Adapting *Into Literature***

Making *Into Literature* Work for You

38   **Flexibility & Choice**

40   Planning the Year

44   Adapting Units of Instruction

48   Teaching with Novels and Longer Works

52   **Student Engagement**

54   Igniting Student Engagement

58   Integrating Social & Emotional Learning

64   **Close Reading & Analysis**

66   Using Notice & Note for Close Reading

72   Developing the Habits of Close Reading

76   **Outcomes & Growth**

78   Building Better Writers

84   Integrating Speaking & Listening

88   Integrating Grammar and Vocabulary into Your Lessons

94   Assessing Student Progress & Mastery

98 **Differentiation**

100 Differentiating Instruction
for Students Who Struggle

104 Supporting English Learners

108 Infusing Rigor and Challenge

112 **Purposeful Technology**

114 Getting the Most Out
of Ed: Your Friend in Learning

120 Integrating Technology
into the ELA Classroom

124 Promoting Digital Literacy

128 Making the Most of an Accessible
Learning Experience

132 **Professional Learning**

134 Surviving Your First Year in the Classroom

140 Growing Your Craft with **HMH Literacy
Solutions**™

142 Growing Your Craft with **Teacher's Corner**

Meeting the Needs of ELA Educators

144 *Into Literature* Unit Planning Guides

146 Grade 9

158 Grade 10

ELA Educators, We're Listening

HMH Into Literature was inspired by you—your words, your instructional needs, your pain points, your questions. Here are some of the common threads affecting ELA educators.

Flexibility & Choice

WHAT WE HEARD

"Curriculum and texts are standardized at the district level. Where do I have flexibility and choice?"

"I want to incorporate novels and longer reads into my instruction."

"It's too hard to figure out how any new program can meet my specific needs."

WHAT WE DID

1. ☑ Developed flexible unit and lesson planning resources, built with realistic pacing in mind

2. ☑ Helped you integrate novels, differentiate instruction, and use additional texts for whole-class and independent reading

3. ☑ Made it easier for you to use only those resources or instructional aspects that work for you

Engagement & Cultural Relevance

WHAT WE HEARD

"Students need to see themselves in what they read."

"It's hard work to engage students and get them to want to read."

"I'm used to teaching the classics; I need more contemporary, diverse connections."

WHAT WE DID

1. ☑ Curated high-interest units of culturally diverse texts that high-schoolers will want to read and discuss

2. ☑ Included activities to engage and motivate students and appeal to their varied interests

Student Growth & Outcomes

WHAT WE HEARD

"I don't like doing isolated test prep—I want it built into what we do daily."

"I need to know the best way to cover my state's standards."

WHAT WE DID

1. ☑ Ensured that you can cover all of your state's standards and gave you a road map for doing so

2. ☑ Gave you embedded and frequent practice in the formats of your state's summative test

3. ☑ Made sure that you have multiple ways to assess students' understanding and mastery of the standards

Lack of Time & Support

WHAT WE HEARD

"I'm new to the profession. Help!"

"Teacher burnout is real. It's never been harder to be a classroom teacher."

"There is simply not enough time to support all the student needs in my classes."

WHAT WE DID

1. ☑ Offered you the same scaffolding, tips, and strategies that we give to students; from first-year teachers to veterans, we want you to feel that "you've got this"

2. ☑ Gave you frequent insights into how your students are doing and recommended resources that can help them, no matter the need

3. ☑ Saved you time through data insights and resource suggestions

Writing

WHAT WE HEARD

"I need more ideas for giving meaningful feedback rather than formally grading everything."

"How do I effectively teach my students how to write?"

"Students need more practice with the kinds of writing they encounter on high-stakes assessments."

WHAT WE DID

1. ☑ Provided more writing activities, prompts, and support—including both creative writing and writing modeled after summative assessments

2. ☑ Gave you access to Writable with digital tools, such as Turn It In, peer review, and Revision Aid, to ease some of the burden on you when grading student work

3. ☑ Tried to demystify teaching writing, so that you have the support you need to guide your students

Integrated Social & Emotional Learning

WHAT WE HEARD

"There is a big push for social-emotional learning in my district. How do I work it in?"

"We have a polarized culture. How do I navigate classroom conversations about difficult topics and texts?"

WHAT WE DID

1. ☑ Included more provocative texts worth debating—and gave you support for facilitating respectful discussions in class

2. ☑ Connected social and emotional learning activities and instruction into each lesson

Effective Use of Technology

WHAT WE HEARD

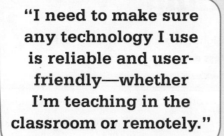

"I need to make sure any technology I use is reliable and user-friendly—whether I'm teaching in the classroom or remotely."

"My school has a learning management system. Show me how your resources can plug into what I am already using."

"I need more support for meaningful integration of technology."

WHAT WE DID

1. ☑ Made all core content available online and offline (through our offline app), providing you with the flexibility to teach in the classroom or remotely

2. ☑ Gave tips, support, and ideas for implementing a blended-learning classroom and teaching remotely

3. ☑ Built in point-of-use tips and recommendations for incorporating digital resources

4. ☑ Provided all texts in printable format and assessments in editable format, giving you more flexibility for offline usage

5. ☑ Made it easier for you to integrate with other systems and tools, like Google Classroom

Connecting Your Expertise and *Into Literature* . . .

We've got this.

Introducing
HMH Into Literature

Connected Teaching

HMH Into Literature offers rich content, actionable insights, personalized learning, and standards-based instruction—**all within one seamless experience**. With HMH's system of connected solutions, you and your students have access to

- assessments that pinpoint learning gaps, as well as driving content and grouping recommendations
- instruction that provides the flexibility for whole-class, small-group, and independent, personalized learning
- professional learning that is embedded within the instruction and available to enrich and enhance the classroom experience

HMH Into Literature provides the instructional tools, rich pedagogy, and professional services to ensure that you and your students not only reach—but exceed—your instructional goals.

Rich Content and Standards-Based Instruction

- Research-based, explicit, and systematic instruction
- Resources and support for whole-class, small-group, and independent work
- Materials for striving readers and writers, English learners, and advanced learners

Assessments and Actionable Insights

- Embedded formative and summative assessments
- Growth Measure reports that help inform instructional decisions, planning, and grouping

Professional Learning

- **Getting Started** for every teacher
- Curated, on-demand, curriculum-aligned content through **Teacher's Corner**
- Online team coaching tailored to your learning needs

Supplemental Digital Practice and Instruction

- Personalized reading practice to address skills diversity
- Writing practice and feedback with customizable assignments that support *HMH Into Literature*

Writable

Program
at a Glance

Overview

Here is everything you need to make *HMH Into Literature* work in your classroom.

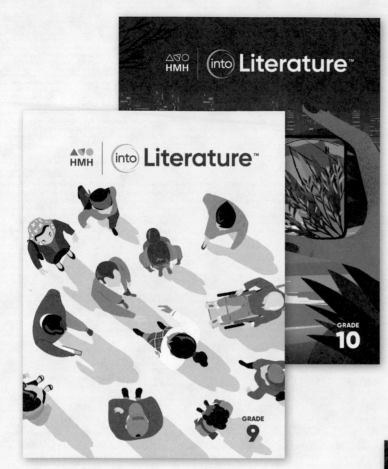

In each grade, a consumable **Student Edition** provides high-interest units and text sets. Wrapped around those texts are instruction and practice in key skills. **Notice & Note** protocol for close reading is also integrated into each lesson.

A **Teacher's Edition** provides point-of-use instructional support and differentiation. It outlines how you can make each unit and lesson your own, using the resources in a way that works best for your classroom.

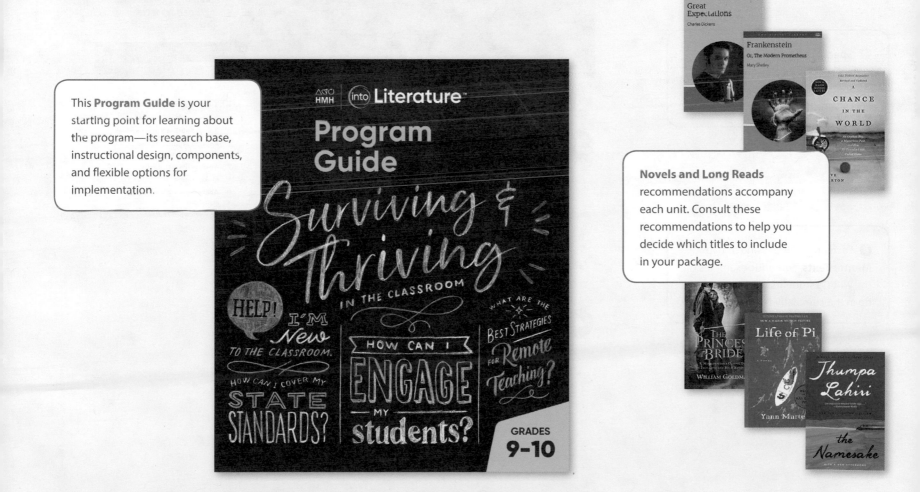

Ed: Your Friend in Learning provides resources and functionality for flexible teaching and meaningful, interactive learning. Find:

- student eBooks with audio, video, annotation, and note-taking functions
- assessments and practice that mirror high-stakes assessment formats
- lesson-planning tools
- data insights on student growth and proficiency, along with recommendations

This **Program Guide** is your starting point for learning about the program—its research base, instructional design, components, and flexible options for implementation.

Novels and Long Reads recommendations accompany each unit. Consult these recommendations to help you decide which titles to include in your package.

Unit at a Glance

Each unit follows a consistent instructional design, grounded in a gradual-release model that moves students from whole-class learning to peer collaboration to independence.

1 Each unit in *Into Literature* focuses on a **high-interest topic** and **Essential Question**, which students explore through different genres.

2 **Spark Your Learning** features activities and prompts for engaging students and building their topic knowledge.

6 Each unit includes one or two **Mentor Texts**, authentic examples of the writing students will be asked to do in the cumulative task.

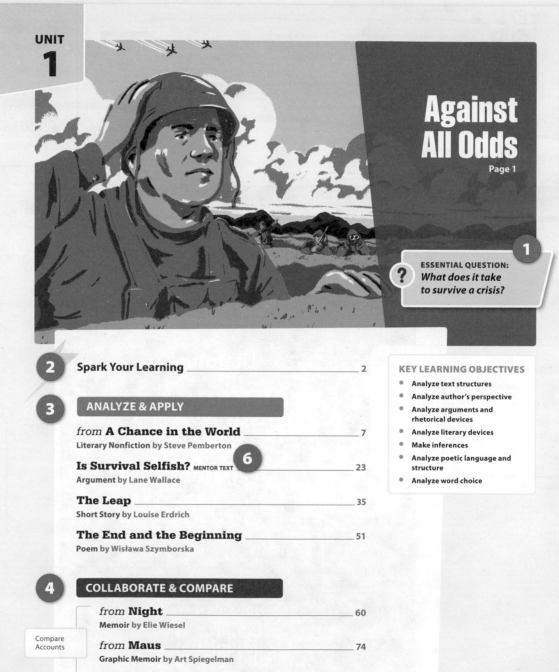

UNIT 1

Against All Odds
Page 1

? **ESSENTIAL QUESTION:** **1**
What does it take to survive a crisis?

2 Spark Your Learning _____ 2

3 **ANALYZE & APPLY**

from **A Chance in the World** _____ 7
Literary Nonfiction by Steve Pemberton

Is Survival Selfish? MENTOR TEXT **6** _____ 23
Argument by Lane Wallace

The Leap _____ 35
Short Story by Louise Erdrich

The End and the Beginning _____ 51
Poem by Wisława Szymborska

4 **COLLABORATE & COMPARE**

Compare Accounts

from **Night** _____ 60
Memoir by Elie Wiesel

from **Maus** _____ 74
Graphic Memoir by Art Spiegelman

KEY LEARNING OBJECTIVES

- Analyze text structures
- Analyze author's perspective
- Analyze arguments and rhetorical devices
- Analyze literary devices
- Make inferences
- Analyze poetic language and structure
- Analyze word choice

Units are divided into three sections:

❸ Analyze & Apply—perfect for whole-class learning

❹ Collaborate & Compare—for peer and small-group work

❺ Reader's Choice—short and long reads for independent reading

UNIT **1**

❺ READER'S CHOICE

Preview the Choices _____ 84

SHORT READS

Adventurers Change. Danger Does Not.
Article by Alan Cowell

from **An Ordinary Man**
Memoir by Paul Rusesabagina

Who Understands Me But Me
Poem by Jimmy Santiago Baca

Truth at All Costs
Speech by Marie Colvin

from **Deep Survival**
Informational Text by Laurence Gonzales

Available online

🖰**Ed**

LONG READS

Night
Memoir
Elie Wiesel

**Enchanted Air:
Two Cultures,
Two Wings**
Memoir
Margarita Engle

Bad Boy
Memoir
Walter Dean Myers

Recommendations

❼ **End-of-unit tasks** in writing and speaking and listening allow students to demonstrate their understanding of learning objectives and offer new insights into the Essential Question.

Writable

All writing prompts, including unit tasks, are available to assign within **Writable**.

❼ UNIT 1 TASKS

WRITING
Write an Argument _____ 86

SPEAKING & LISTENING
Present and Respond to an Argument _____ 95

REFLECT & EXTEND _____ 97

🖰**Ed**

Go online for
Unit and Selection Videos
Interactive Annotation and Text Analysis
Selection Audio Recordings
Collaborative Writing   Writable

Lesson at a Glance

Each lesson also follows a consistent structure, with activities and instruction occurring before, during, and after reading. Take a closer look at each section on the following pages.

Get Ready

Each lesson opens with a **Get Ready** feature, which provides activities, background, and instruction that prepare students for reading.

Instructional Features:

1. Engage Your Brain
2. Skills-Based Instruction
3. Annotation in Action
4. Expand Your Vocabulary
5. Background

Get Ready

from
A Chance in the World
Literary Nonfiction by Steve Pemberton

ESSENTIAL QUESTION:
What does it take to survive a crisis?

Engage Your Brain ①

Choose one or more of these activities to start connecting with the text you're about to read.

Does Everyone Have a Chance?

Think about the title of this text. Does everyone have the same chances and opportunities to be successful in life?

1. In the appropriate column of the T-chart, list ways and reasons people do or do not have the same opportunities for success in life.

2. Discuss your conclusions with a partner.

Yes	No

Sources of Strength

We can draw on sources of strength and support when we find ourselves in a dangerous or painful situation. For example, we may turn to a trusted friend or adult. Make a list of ways people can cope with threatening or even perilous situations.

These Are a Few of My Favorite Things

Think back to when you were younger. What were your "comfort" items—things, activities, or places that made you happy or perhaps took you to another world? Sketch pictures or make a list.

Get Ready

Analyze Literary Nonfiction ②

Literary nonfiction conveys factual information, ideas, or experiences using literary techniques. Literary nonfiction can include memoirs such as *A Chance in the World* as well as autobiographies, biographies, and speeches. How can you tell the difference between literary nonfiction and other informational texts?

- Look for lyrical or even poetic descriptions that go beyond simple explanations.
- Notice **figurative language** (for example, similes and metaphors) and **sensory details** (words and phrases appealing to the senses).
- Take note of how the author interprets what he or she is describing or experiencing.
- Watch for the author's reflections on the meaning of experiences.

Focus on Genre
↳ **Literary Nonfiction**

- conveys factual information, ideas, or experiences
- develops insights that go beyond the facts
- uses literary devices such as figurative and sensory language

---

Get Ready

Annotation in Action ③

Here is an example of notes a student made about a passage from *A Chance in the World.* As you read, mark words and phrases that convey details about the author's situation.

> One way I dealt with these monsters was to become a thief, and a very good one at that. My devious plots were elaborate, complete with escape routes and explanations if I were to get caught.

"Monsters!"– the Robinsons must be awful.

Amazing what he does to cope.

Expand Your Vocabulary ④

Put a check mark next to the vocabulary words that you feel comfortable using when speaking or writing.

- fathom ☐
- thwart ☐
- cacophony ☐
- sanctuary ☐
- baffle ☐

Using the words you already know, work with a partner to write a paragraph about someone who is in a place that feels unsafe or threatening.

As you read the excerpt from *A Chance in the World,* use the definitions in the side column to help you learn the vocabulary words you don't already know.

A Chance in the World
…be the Robinsons

Background ⑤

Steve Pemberton was born and raised in New Bedford, Massachusetts. After graduating from Boston College with degrees in political science and sociology, he worked as a college admissions officer and then embarked on a career as an executive at Monster.com, Walgreens, and Workhuman. Pemberton's memoir, *A Chance in the World,* was published in 2012. He says he wrote it in part because "I wanted to contribute to the universal story of family, faith, fortitude, and forgiveness."

Read

As students read, they are prompted to annotate and analyze the text carefully.

Instructional Features:

6 Standards-Based Guided Reading Questions with Annotation

7 Notice & Note Signposts

8 Vocabulary in Context

9 Assessment Practice

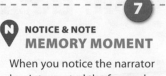

7

NOTICE & NOTE
MEMORY MOMENT

When you notice the narrator has interrupted the forward progress of a story by bringing up something from the past, you've found a **Memory Moment** signpost.

Notice & Note: Mark the lines in paragraph 29 that tell about something that happened in the past.

Analy
memo

6

ANALYZE AUTHOR'S PERSPECTIVE

Annotate: Mark the sentence in paragraph 9 that reveals what Steve wonders about most.

Infer: What does this suggest about Steve's sense of identity?

9

Assessment Practice

Answer these questions before moving on to the **Analyze the Text** section on the following page.

1. Select **two** strategies Steve uses to cope with his situation.
   - (A) sneaking food
   - (B) running away
   - (C) reading
   - (D) taking walks
   - (E) staying with the Levins

2. How does paragraph 32 contribute to the development of the author's ideas?
   - (A) by emphasizing the importance of having a challenging reading list
   - (B) by providing details of the author's escape into the world of books
   - (C) by describing how his books were gradually destroyed
   - (D) by describing his secret reading place in the cellar

3. This question has two parts. First, answer **Part A**. Then, answer **Part B**.

   Part A
   Which statement best describes the purpose of this text?
   - (A) to demonstrate the cruelty of the Robinsons
   - (B) to describe the books Steve read during this time
   - (C) to describe how Steve confronted and overcame hardships
   - (D) to show how the American foster system works

   Part B
   Select the sentence that best supports the answer to Part A.
   - (A) "Children rarely ask wh
   - (B) "...this little boy does
   - (C) "Caseworkers at the ti
   - (D) "Mrs. Levin's books ga

A Chance in the World 15

8

baffle

(băf´əl) *v.* to confuse or perplex.

Respond

After reading, students respond to the text in a variety of ways.

Instructional Features:

10 Analyze the Text Questions

11 Choices

12 Expand Your Vocabulary

13 Watch Your Language!

10

Respond

Analyze the Text

Support your responses with evidence from the text.

1. **INTERPRET** Review the chart you completed on the Get Ready page. How would you describe the author's perspective on this period of his life?

2. **ANALYZE** Identify two or three "Robinson rules." How do you know there are many such rules? How does this fact add to the author's portrayal of this period in his life?

3. **INFER** The author describes a wall "as if hewn from the side of a mountain." Find other examples of figurative language. Why did the author not confine himself to a factual recounting of events?

4. **EVALUATE** Deception, cunning, trickery, thieving: Steve boasts about his abilities to deceive and outwit the Robinsons. Who or what is Steve's model? How does he justify his own deceptions?

5. **ANALYZE** What sensory language—descriptions that appeal to the senses—does the author use? Cite two or three examples. What does this language tell you about the narrator's perceptions?

NOTICE & NOTE
Review what you **noticed and noted** as you read the text. Your annotations can help you answer these questions.

11

Choices

Here are some other ways to demonstrate your understanding of the ideas in this lesson.

Writing
↳ **Personal Reflection**

Author Steve Pemberton describes several significant personal experiences in this excerpt from his memoir. These experiences, and his reactions to them, shaped the person he later became. Think about one experience you would be comfortable sharing that has shaped your life. Then freewrite about it. Include relevant information such as:

- a description of the experience
- who was involved besides you
- how it affected or changed you

Endure His Situation

Speaking
↳ Deb

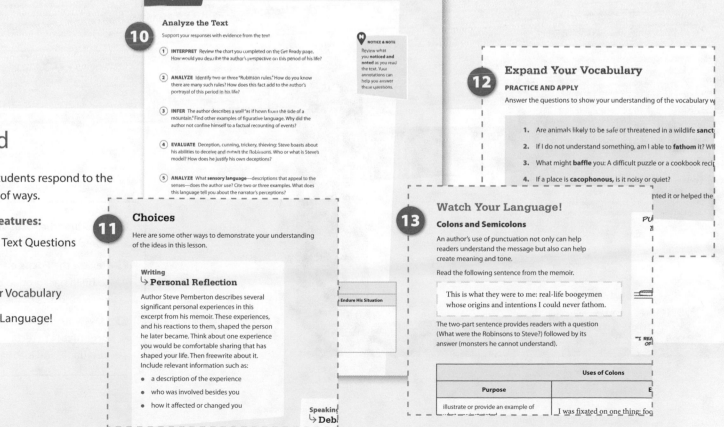

12

Expand Your Vocabulary

PRACTICE AND APPLY

Answer the questions to show your understanding of the vocabulary w

1. Are animals likely to be safe or threatened in a wildlife **sanct**
2. If I do not understand something, am I able to **fathom** it? Wh
3. What might **baffle** you: A difficult puzzle or a cookbook recip
4. If a place is **cacophonous**, is it noisy or quiet?

nted it or helped the

13

Watch Your Language!

Colons and Semicolons

An author's use of punctuation not only can help readers understand the message but also can help create meaning and tone.

Read the following sentence from the memoir.

> This is what they were to me: real-life boogeymen whose origins and intentions I could never fathom.

The two-part sentence provides readers with a question (What were the Robinsons to Steve?) followed by its answer (monsters he cannot understand).

Uses of Colons	
Purpose	**E**
illustrate or provide an example of	I was fixated on one thing: fo

---

Teaching a Lesson: Get Ready

① Use the quick **Engage Your Brain** activities to motivate your students and get them talking and writing about key ideas related to each text.

Analyze Literary Nonfiction **②**

Literary nonfiction conveys factual information, ideas, or experiences using literary techniques. Literary nonfiction can include memoirs such as *A Chance in the World* as well as autobiographies, biographies, and speeches. How can you tell the difference between literary nonfiction and other informational texts?

- Look for lyrical or even poetic descriptions that go beyond simple explanations.
- Notice **figurative language** (for example, similes and metaphors) and **sensory details** (words and phrases appealing to the senses).
- Take note of how the author interprets what he or she is describing or experiencing.
- Watch for the author's reflections on the meaning of experiences.

In this memoir, author Steve Pemberton recalls a traumatic time in his childhood—and shares where he found comfort and strength. As you read, notice the language the author uses to communicate the impact of his experiences. Also think about why he might have chosen to include particular events and details.

③

Focus on Genre
↳ **Literary Nonfiction**

- conveys factual information, ideas, or experiences
- develops insights that go beyond the facts
- uses literary devices such as figurative and sensory language

Analyze Author's Perspective

An **author's perspective,** or point of view, is a unique combination of ideas, values, feelings, and beliefs that influences the way the writer looks at a topic. Authors reveal their perspectives in a variety of ways. One clue is the author's **diction,** or choice of words. Authors also communicate their perspective through the details they choose to focus on and direct statements about their feelings and beliefs.

As you read the text, fill out the chart to help you understand Steve Pemberton's perspective on this particular period in his childhood.

Clues to Author's Perspective	Examples from *A Chance in the World*
Language (diction)	"monsters" used to describe the Robinsons
Details the author includes	**④**
Direct statements about the author's feelings and beliefs	

---

from
A Chance in the World

Literary Nonfiction by **Steve Pemberton**

? ESSENTIAL QUESTION:
What does it take to survive a crisis?

Engage Your Brain **①**

Choose one or more of these activities to start connecting with the text you're about to read.

Sources of Strength

We can draw on sources of strength and support when we find ourselves in a dangerous or painful situation. For example, we may turn to a trusted friend or adult. Make a list of ways people can cope with threatening or even perilous situations.

Does Everyone Have a Chance?

Think about the title of this text. Does everyone have the same chances and opportunities to be successful in life?

1. In the appropriate column of the T-chart, list ways and reasons people do or do not have the same opportunities for success in life.
2. Discuss your conclusions with a partner.

Yes	No

These Are a Few of My Favorite Things

Think back to when you were younger. What were your "comfort" items—things, activities, or places that made you happy or perhaps took you to another world? Sketch pictures or make a list.

② Introduce the **focus skills and standards** covered in the lesson.

③ Review the **Focus on Genre** to build background on the characteristics of the genre.

④ Have your students use the **graphic organizers** to record key details, language, and ideas as they read.

Get Ready

Annotation in Action (5)

Here is an example of notes a student made about a passage from *A Chance in the World*. As you read, mark words and phrases that convey details about the author's situation.

> One way I dealt with these monsters was to become a thief, and a very good one at that. My devious plots were elaborate, complete with escape routes and explanations if I were to get caught.

"Monsters!"– the Robinsons must be awful.

Amazing what he does to cope.

Expand Your Vocabulary

Put a check mark next to the vocabulary words that you feel comfortable using when speaking or writing.

(6)

fathom	☐
thwart	☐
cacophony	☐
sanctuary	☐
baffle	☐

Using the words you already know, work with a partner to write a paragraph about someone who is in a place that feels unsafe or threatening.

As you read the excerpt from *A Chance in the World*, use the definitions in the side column to help you learn the vocabulary words you don't already know.

Background (7)

Steve Pemberton was born and raised in New Bedford, Massachusetts. After graduating from Boston College with degrees in political science and sociology, he worked as a college admissions officer and then embarked on a career as an executive at Monster.com, Walgreens, and Workhuman. Pemberton's memoir, *A Chance in the World*, was published in 2012. He says he wrote it in part because "I wanted to contribute to the universal story of family, faith, fortitude, and forgiveness."

6   UNIT 1   **ANALYZE & APPLY**

Company • Image Credits: © Jean Allen · Gibosa/Houghton Mifflin Harcourt

---

(5) As a class, discuss **Annotation in Action** to reinforce what effective close reading looks like.

(6) See which **vocabulary words** students already know.

(7) **Build background** about the author, setting, or topic.

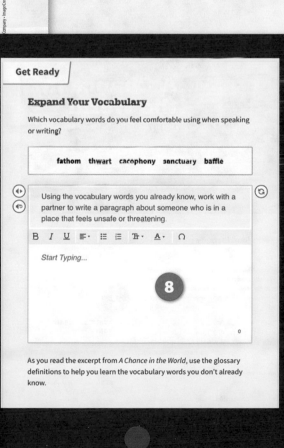

(8) Project the **Digital Student Edition** as you work through the activities as a class, or assign activities to small groups or individuals.

Teaching a Lesson: Read

❶ Use the **Notice & Note** annotations and questions to sharpen students' reading and text analysis. Learn more about the Notice & Note protocol on pages 66–71.

from

A Chance in the World

Literary Nonfiction by **Steve Pemberton**

A young boy in foster care seeks food for body and soul.

Steve Pemberton became an orphan at age three when it became clear that his birth parents could not care for him. After being moved through several foster homes, Steve was finally placed with the Robinson family in New Bedford, Massachusetts, which is the setting for this excerpt. The "Robinson rules" refer to harsh regulations his foster parents imposed.

NOTICE & NOTE
As you read, use the side margins to make notes about the text.

> *"All the world will be your enemy, Prince of a Thousand Enemies, and whenever they catch you, they will kill you. But first they must catch you, digger, listener, runner, prince with the swift warning. Be cunning and full of tricks . . ."*
> Richard Adams, *Watership Down*

1   I settled into a routine at the house on Arnold Street, to the degree one can ever become comfortable with monsters who disguise themselves as human beings. This is what they were to me: real-life boogeymen whose origins and intentions I could never **fathom**. Children rarely ask where monsters come from or how they came to be; children simply accept them as a fact of life, something to be dealt with, the way you deal with any other childhood fear.

2

ANALYZE LITERARY NONFICTION

Annotate: Mark the figurative language in paragraph 32. What types of figurative language are used here?

Analyze: What shelters the narrator? Who or what is threatening him?

fathom
(făth´əm) *v.* to comprehend.

A Chance in the World   **7**

---

25   "Whoa," I said.
26   "These," she said, "are for the boy who likes to read."
27   "Thank you, ma'am," I said, barely able to take my eyes off the box. "You're welcome," she said, smiling; and with that, she left. She was barely out of earshot before Betty's voice boomed, 'Take those books downstairs! I better never see them up here."
28   "Yes, ma'am, right now, ma'am," I stammered. I feared that she would make me throw them away.
29   Nothing I write can accurately capture the power and timeliness of the gift Mrs. Levin gave me that day. Though I did not know it at the time, several years earlier, when I was one and a half years old, a babysitter had written: "Dropped Steve off at the latest family his mother is boarding him out to . . . he cried his heart out . . . this little boy doesn't have a chance in the world." Others believed this as well, especially those to whose care I was entrusted. I sensed it in their sidelong glances and empathetic shakes of the head, their eyes saying what their tongues would not. *You are beyond repair.*

1

NOTICE & NOTE
MEMORY MOMENT

When you notice the narrator has interrupted the forward progress of a story by bringing up something from the past, you've found a **Memory Moment** signpost.

Notice & Note: Mark the lines in paragraph 29 that tell about something that happened in the past.

Analyze: Why might this memory be important?

12   UNIT 1   **ANALYZE & APPLY**

---

❷ Have students answer the **Guided Reading Questions** in the margins to practice what they learned about the focus skills.

ANALYZE AUTHOR'S PERSPECTIVE

Annotate: Mark the sentence in paragraph 34 where the author states a belief.

Interpret: What does this belief suggest about Steve's view of the world?

34 The rabbits escape the farm and often resort to trickery in their pursuit of a new home. Deception may seem unprincipled, but it is absolutely necessary if Hazel and his group of rabbits are to survive, especially when their very existence is threatened by another group of rabbits, the Efrafrans, and their evil leader, General Woundwort. There comes a time when deception is not enough, and the group must take a stand against General Woundwort, although they know it will likely cost them their lives.

35 I found kinship in the rabbits of *Watership Down*. They became my childhood friends, the only ones I was allowed to have, and I could cite their names at the drop of a hat: Fiver, Bigwig, Pipkin, and Blackberry. My friends were smart, fast, elusive, and resourceful—their very survival was predicated on their ability to sense danger. Though confronted by bigger foes, they outwitted them. Perhaps most important, I saw the rabbits as fighters, their combativeness driven by a certainty that they could create a different and better life for themselves. For Hazel and his followers, it was never a question of *if* they would find a home; it was simply a matter of *when*.

ANALYZE LITERARY NONFICTION

Annotate: Mark the sentences in paragraph 36 where the author is reflecting on Mrs. Levin.

Interpret: What does Steve mean by the metaphor that books would "sow the seeds of my rebellion"?

36 Over the years, Mrs. Levin stopped by many times to deliver a new box of books. In my quiet moments of reflection, I often wonder what might have become of me had not this kind woman lit a pathway for me through the suffocating darkness of the house on Arnold Street. The Robinsons never refused her request, perhaps because they knew that would raise suspicions. But had they known those books would sow the seeds of my rebellion, they would have torched them the minute Mrs. Levin was out of their sight.

? ESSENTIAL QUESTION:
What does it take to survive a crisis?

4

Review your notes and add your thoughts to your Response Log

COLLABORATIVE DISCUSSION **3**

Based on this excerpt, what is the single most important factor in making Steve feel like he has "a chance in the world"? Discuss your opinion with a partner.

3 Prompt meaningful discussion by using the **Collaborative Discussion** activity.

4 Have students revisit the **Essential Question**, recording evidence from the text in their Response Logs, which are located in the back of the Student Edition and online.

5 Use the **annotation and note-taking tools** in the **eBook** to model close reading and generate class discussion.

6 Check students' comprehension of the text with the **Assessment Practice** feature.

Assessment Practice

Answer these questions before moving on to the **Analyze the Text** section on the following page.

1. Select **two** strategies Steve uses to cope with his situation.

6

- (A) sneaking food
- (B) running away
- (C) reading
- (D) taking walks
- (E) staying with the Levins

2. How does paragraph 32 contribute to the development of the author's ideas?

- (A) by emphasizing the importance of having a challenging reading list
- (B) by providing details of the author's escape into the world of books
- (C) by describing how his books were gradually destroyed
- (D) by describing his secret reading place in the cellar

3. This question has two parts. First, answer **Part A**. Then, answer **Part B**.

Part A

Which statement best describes the purpose of this text?

- (A) to demonstrate the cruelty of the Robinsons
- (B) to describe the books Steve read during this time
- (C) to describe how Steve confronted and overcame hardships
- (D) to show how the American foster system works

Part B

Select the sentence that best supports the answer to Part A.

- (A) "Children rarely ask where monsters come from or how they came to be . . ."
- (B) ". . . this little boy doesn't have a chance in the world."
- (C) "Caseworkers at the time described me as tense, nervous, and anxious."
- (D) "Mrs. Levin's books gave me . . . a model for dealing with the Robinsons."

15

manner that fully revealed her **apprehension** 💬 . She was an apt woman; and a little experience soon demonstrated, to her satisfaction, that education and slavery were incompatible with each other.

5

3 From this time I was most narrowly watched. If I was in a separate room any ...th of time, I was sure to aving a book, and was at e an account of myself. was too late. The first en. Mistress, in teaching had given me the inch, could prevent me from taking the *ell*.

These sentences help to show the considerable scrutiny that the author was under at all times. He had to be careful of being discovered.

View in Panel | Save and Close

ANALYZE AUTOBIOGRAPHY

Annotate: Highlight details in paragraph 2 that describe Douglass's mistress.

Infer: Highlight *this* question text and add your responses as a note.

What might Douglass's purpose be in devoting so much space to describing his mistress?

Teaching a Lesson: Respond

Respond

Analyze the Text

Support your responses with evidence from the text.

(1) **INTERPRET** Review the chart you completed on the Get Ready page. How would you describe the author's perspective on this period of his life?

(2) **ANALYZE** Identify two or three "Robinson rules." How do you know there are many such rules? How does this fact add to the author's portrayal of this period in his life?

(3) **INFER** The author describes a wall "as if hewn from the side of a mountain." Find other examples of figurative language. Why did the author not confine himself to a factual recounting of events?

(4) **EVALUATE** Deception, cunning, trickery, thieving: Steve boasts about his abilities to deceive and outwit the Robinsons. Who or what is Steve's model? How does he justify his own deceptions?

(5) **ANALYZE** What **sensory language**—descriptions that appeal to the senses—does the author use? Cite two or three examples. What does this language tell you about the narrator's perceptions?

(6) **SYNTHESIZE** Review the **Memory Moment** in paragraph 29. How do Mrs. Levin's actions provide Steve with the "chance" the babysitter and others were sure he didn't have?

(7) **CONNECT** How does this memoir excerpt address the unit's Essential Question, What does it take to survive a crisis? Use the graphic organizer to record strategies Steve uses to survive, physically and emotionally, in the Robinson household.

N NOTICE & NOTE
Review what you **noticed and noted** as you read the text. Your annotations can help you answer these questions.

Essential Question: What does it take to survive a crisis?	
Coping Mechanism or Source of Support	**How It Helps Steve Endure His Situation**

16   UNIT 1   **ANALYZE & APPLY**

---

1 Have students use their annotations to complete the **Analyze the Text** questions, which reinforce understanding of the focus skills.

2 Use the **Choices** activities to extend students' analysis of the text. Find a range of options, including writing, media production, speaking and listening, research, and social and emotional learning.

Respond

2 Choices

Here are some other ways to demonstrate your understanding of the ideas in this lesson.

Writing
↳ **Personal Reflection**

Author Steve Pemberton describes several significant personal experiences in this excerpt from his memoir. These experiences, and his reactions to them, shaped the person he later became. Think about one experience you would be comfortable sharing that has shaped your life. Then freewrite about it. Include relevant information such as:

● a description of the experience

● who was involved besides you

● how it affected or changed you

As you write and discuss, be sure to use the **Academic Vocabulary** words.

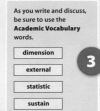

| dimension |
| external |
| statistic |
| sustain |
| utilize |

3

Social & Emotional Learning
↳ **Tribute**

Create a video or illustrated booklet describing a person, group, or organization that has had a positive effect on your life. Include the following information:

● background or description of the person(s) or organization

● how and why the connection occurred

● how your life has changed as a result

Speaking & Listening
↳ **Debate**

Some schools require students to complete volunteer hours in addition to their regular class work. Those schools believe students are improving their communities and learning important life lessons. Others believe that to require volunteering makes it less meaningful. Research the topic, then organize a debate about whether schools should require students to volunteer.

1. Organize two groups: one in favor of mandatory volunteer work, the other opposed.

2. Each side will choose a representative to state the group's opinion.

3. Each side should argue their position using evidence and reasons.

4. Debaters should use appropriate register (degree of formality) and tone.

5. Members should listen and respond to other arguments, identifying any faulty reasoning or distorted evidence.

6. Together, the two sides should review the ideas discussed and summarize conclusions.

A Chance in the World   17

---

3 Challenge students to use **Academic Vocabulary** in their writing and discussions.

© Houghton Mifflin Publishing Company

> 4 Assign the **Vocabulary Practice** to help students master key words from the text.
>
> 5 Teach the **Vocabulary Strategy**, looking back at the text for context.

Expand Your Vocabulary

PRACTICE AND APPLY

Answer the questions to show your understanding of the vocabulary words.

1. Are animals likely to be safe or threatened in a wildlife **sanctuary**?

2. If I do not understand something, am I able to **fathom** it? Why?

3. What might **baffle** you: A difficult puzzle or a cookbook recipe?

4. If a place is **cacophonous**, is it noisy or quiet?

5. If I **thwart** someone's plan, have I prevented it or helped the person achieve it?

Vocabulary Strategy
↳ **Patterns of Word Changes** 5

You have probably noticed that many words can change form to become new words with related meanings. When you learn the common patterns of word changes, you can recognize different forms of familiar words and figure out what they mean. Knowing the patterns will also help you spell different forms of a word correctly.

The word *precisely* in paragraphs 5 and 7 is an adverb meaning "exactly." Adding the suffix *-ion* creates the noun *precision*. Removing *-ly* creates the adjective *precise*. Adding the prefix *im-* creates the word *imprecise*, meaning "not exact."

Ed
Interactive Vocabulary Lesson: Analyzing Word Structure

Verb	Noun	Adjective	Adverb
explain	explanation	explainable	
frequent	frequency	frequent	frequently
create	creation/creativity	creative	creatively

PRACTICE AND APPLY

- For each verb in the chart, identify one new verb that has the same ending (*-ain, -ent, -ate*).
- Create a chart with your words in the first column.
- Complete the chart with noun and adjective forms of each word.
- Choose one word from each row of your chart and use it in a sentence.

Watch Your Language! 6

Colons and Semicolons

An author's use of punctuation not only can help readers understand the message but also can help create meaning and tone.

Read the following sentence from the memoir.

> This is what they were to me: real-life boogeymen whose origins and intentions I could never fathom.

The two-part sentence provides readers with a question (What were the Robinsons to Steve?) followed by its answer (monsters he cannot understand).

PUNCTUATION RULES THE SEMI-COLON

"I REALIZE THAT MOST OF YOU THINK THE FUNCTION OF THE SEMI-COLON IS TO MAKE A *WINKING SMILEY FACE* WHEN TEXTING . . ."

Uses of Colons	
Purpose	**Example**
illustrate or provide an example of what was just stated	I was fixated on one thing: food.
introduce a quotation or dialogue	But Mrs. Levin was insistent: "If it's okay, I would like to give him these myself."
introduce a list	And my hearing was finely tuned. I knew the stride pattern of each member of the family: Betty shuffled, Reggie had longer steps, and Willie's plodding was the easiest to detect. . . .

Author Steve Pemberton also uses semicolons effectively. Here is another sentence from *A Chance in the World*:

> For Hazel and his followers, it was never a question of *if* they would find a home; it was simply a matter of *when*.

The author's use of the semicolon shows the relationship between the two statements.

Ed
Interactive Grammar Lesson: Colons

PRACTICE AND APPLY 7

With a partner, write a paragraph about whether you think Steve's deceptions were justified given his living conditions at the Robinsons. Use colons and semicolons in at least three places. At least one colon should provide an example of the first part of the statement; and at least one semicolon should come before a conjunctive adverb (*however, nevertheless, also*).

> 6 Use the **Watch Your Language!** feature to teach grammar in context.
>
> 7 Assign the **Practice** and find more practice online.

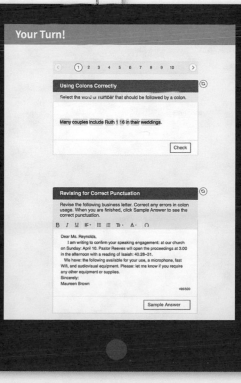

Your Turn!

< 1 2 3 4 5 6 7 8 9 10 >

Using Colons Correctly

Select the word or number that should be followed by a colon.

Many couples include Ruth 1 16 in their weddings.

Check

Revising for Correct Punctuation

Revise the following business letter. Correct any errors in colon usage. When you are finished, click Sample Answer to see the correct punctuation.

B I U S · ≡ ≡ T · A · Ω

Dear Ms. Reynolds,
   I am writing to confirm your speaking engagement: at our church on Sunday: April 10. Pastor Reeves will open the proceedings at 3.00 in the afternoon with a reading of Isaiah: 40.28–31.
   We have the following available for your use, a microphone, fast WiFi, and audiovisual equipment. Please: let me know if you require any other equipment or supplies.
Sincerely:
Maureen Brown

Sample Answer

Adapting
Into Literature

Teacher's Edition

No two educators will approach *Into Literature* in the same way. You can customize what's here to work for you, your school, and most importantly, your students. The articles in the next section of this guide will help you adapt this program to your needs. Here is a preview of some of the core and supporting resources that allow for flexibility and choice, starting with your Teacher's Edition.

Unit Planning Guides

All the **Unit Planning Guides** for your grade level are available in the back of this guide, on pages 146–169. Consult these materials as you plan and adapt your curriculum for the unit or year.

Instructional Features:

1. Find information about **realistic pacing** and **text complexity** for each lesson in the unit.

2. View **standards** covered in each lesson.

3. Discover **online resources** to support your instruction.

4. Preview **independent reading options** connected to the unit.

5. See **options for assessing mastery** of unit standards and skills.

Want specific ideas for integrating longer works into your teaching? Find practical suggestions and resources on pages 48–51.

Instructional Features:

6 Discover **Short Reads** that connect to the unit, should you want to make any changes to the default lessons or texts.

7 Use the tips to find instructional resources that can pair with these texts.

8 Use the **Long Reads** suggestions to help you integrate novels and other longer works into the unit. You will find five recommendations for each unit.

UNIT 1 ⌾Ed

Flexible Short Read Options

What if I want to use a different text? ⌾Ed

...because the text is too hard or too easy
Tip Choose a better Lexile match.

...because I don't think my students will like the text
Tip Review student responses to Preview the Texts on p. 3 to gauge their interest.

...because I don't have enough time
Tip Remove it from the unit! Check if there are any assessment items you might want to remove from the Unit Test.

Tips and Tricks! ⌾Ed
Check the **Growth Measure Report** on **Ed** to review students' Lexile proficiency, and consider whether you want to swap out texts that are too hard or too easy for most of the class.

Choose a Text

Choose one of the Reader's Choice **Short Read** texts for this unit. These selections and assessments are only available **online**.

6

Adventurers Change. Danger Does Not. 1160L
Article by Alan Cowell

from An Ordinary Man 980L
Memoir by Paul Rusesabagina

Who Understands Me But Me N/A
Poem by Jimmy Santiago Baca

Truth at All Costs 1060L
Speech by Marie Colvin

from Deep Survival 950L
Informational Text by Laurence Gonzales

— OR —

Search the HMH Text Library for additional selections. Here are some suggestions related to the unit theme:

- **Decide to Survive** (900L)
- **In the Family** (1240L)
- **Niña** (860L)
- **Fight or Flight?** (1150L)
- **Be a Survivor!** (920L)

Choose a Skill

If desired, pair the text with some skills instruction to suit your needs.

- **Skills Coach:** provides skills-based practice with any text
- **Peer Coach Videos:** peers provide skills-based instruction
- **Anchor Charts:** high-level visual summaries of skill instruction

7

⌾Ed

Adjust the Assessment

- Create your own test items on **Ed**.
- Build a practice assessment for the skills you want to teach using the Guided Skills Practice.

---

1 PLANNING GUIDE

Flexible Long Read Options

How can I incorporate a longer work into this unit? ⌾Ed

...for independent reading
Tip Reserve a block of class time for assessments.

...for Literature Circles or groups
Tip Model each role for the students to ensure they are effective contributors.

...for guided reading
Tip Commit significant class time to instruction, comprehension checks, discussions, and projects in addition to reading.

Tips and Tricks! ⌾Ed
- Use an HMH Long Read Study Guide for all suggested books. Study Guides include teacher support, student activities, and assessment.
- You can pair a **Long Read** with **Skills Coach**, **Peer Coach Videos**, and/or **Anchor Charts** for additional skills support.

Choose a Text

Choose one of the recommended **Long Reads** for this unit. The books featured here provide additional opportunities for students to explore the Unit 1 theme and Essential Question in depth.

8

Night
Memoir by Elie Wiesel

Enchanted Air: Two Cultures, Two Wings
Memoir by Margarita Engle

Bad Boy
Memoir by Walter Dean Myers

Connection to the Unit
- **Summary:** Elie Wiesel recounts the horrors he faced as a teenager in the Nazi death camps. He reflects on his will to survive and man's capacity for inhumanity.
- **Pairs with:** If students were moved by the excerpt of *Night* in the unit, they may be interested in reading more about Wiesel's experience in the full book.

Connection to the Unit
- **Summary:** Margarita is a girl from two worlds. With hostility brewing between Cuba and the United States, she wonders if she can still belong to both.
- This memoir will engage students who are interested in the unit topic of surviving a crisis.

Connection to the Unit
- **Summary:** Walter has a quick-temper and is always ready for a fight. He also loves to read and write. How will the streets of Harlem shape him, and who will he become?
- **Pairs with:** In the excerpt of "A Chance in the World," Pemberton faces extreme adversity and hardship to eventually succeed.

Additional Options
A Chance in the World
Literary Nonfiction by Steve Pemberton

The Best We Could Do
Graphic Memoir by Thi Bui

Adjust the Assessment ⌾Ed
Customize the Unit Test on **Ed** to incorporate the longer work.

Adapting *Into Literature*
Teacher's Edition

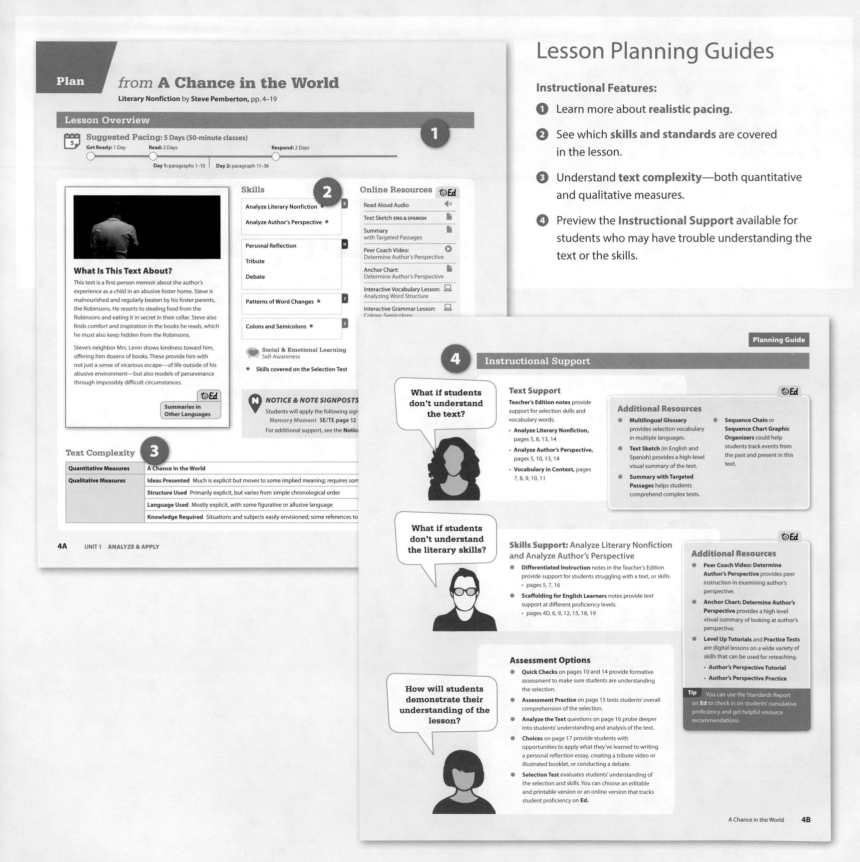

Lesson Planning Guides

Instructional Features:

1. Learn more about **realistic pacing**.

2. See which **skills and standards** are covered in the lesson.

3. Understand **text complexity**—both quantitative and qualitative measures.

4. Preview the **Instructional Support** available for students who may have trouble understanding the text or the skills.

Plan — *from* A Chance in the World
Literary Nonfiction by Steve Pemberton, pp. 4–19

Lesson Overview

Suggested Pacing: 5 Days (50-minute classes)

Get Ready: 1 Day   Read: 2 Days   Respond: 2 Days

Day 1: paragraphs 1–10   Day 2: paragraph 11–36

What Is This Text About?

This text is a first-person memoir about the author's experience as a child in an abusive foster home. Steve is malnourished and regularly beaten by his foster parents, the Robinsons. He resorts to stealing food from the Robinsons and eating it in secret in their cellar. Steve also finds comfort and inspiration in the books he reads, which he must also keep hidden from the Robinsons.

Steve's neighbor Mrs. Levin shows kindness toward him, offering him dozens of books. These provide him with not just a sense of vicarious escape—of life outside of his abusive environment—but also models of perseverance through impossibly difficult circumstances.

Summaries in Other Languages

Skills

Analyze Literary Nonfiction *
Analyze Author's Perspective *

Personal Reflection
Tribute
Debate

Patterns of Word Changes *

Colons and Semicolons *

Social & Emotional Learning
Self-Awareness

* Skills covered on the Selection Test

NOTICE & NOTE SIGNPOSTS
Students will apply the following sign...
Memory Moment SE/TE page 12
For additional support, see the Notic...

Online Resources

Read Aloud Audio
Text Sketch ENG & SPANISH
Summary with Targeted Passages
Peer Coach Video: Determine Author's Perspective
Anchor Chart: Determine Author's Perspective
Interactive Vocabulary Lesson: Analyzing Word Structure
Interactive Grammar Lesson: Colons; Semicolons

Text Complexity

Quantitative Measures	A Chance in the World
Qualitative Measures	**Ideas Presented** Much is explicit but moves to some implied meaning; requires som...
	Structure Used Primarily explicit, but varies from simple chronological order
	Language Used Mostly explicit, with some figurative or allusive language
	Knowledge Required Situations and subjects easily envisioned; some references to...

4A   UNIT 1   ANALYZE & APPLY

Planning Guide

4 Instructional Support

What if students don't understand the text?

Text Support

Teacher's Edition notes provide support for selection skills and vocabulary words.

- **Analyze Literary Nonfiction,** pages 5, 8, 13, 14
- **Analyze Author's Perspective,** pages 5, 10, 13, 14
- **Vocabulary in Context,** pages 7, 8, 9, 10, 11

Additional Resources

- **Multilingual Glossary** provides selection vocabulary in multiple languages.
- **Text Sketch** (in English and Spanish) provides a high-level visual summary of the text.
- **Summary with Targeted Passages** helps students comprehend complex texts.
- **Sequence Chain** or **Sequence Chart Graphic Organizers** could help students track events from the past and present in this text.

What if students don't understand the literary skills?

Skills Support: Analyze Literary Nonfiction and Analyze Author's Perspective

- **Differentiated Instruction** notes in the Teacher's Edition provide support for students struggling with a text, or skills.
  - pages 5, 7, 16
- **Scaffolding for English Learners** notes provide text support at different proficiency levels.
  - pages 4D, 6, 9, 12, 15, 18, 19

Additional Resources

- **Peer Coach Video: Determine Author's Perspective** provides peer instruction in examining author's perspective.
- **Anchor Chart: Determine Author's Perspective** provides a high level visual summary of looking at author's perspective.
- **Level Up Tutorials** and **Practice Tests** are digital lessons on a wide variety of skills that can be used for reteaching.
  - **Author's Perspective Tutorial**
  - **Author's Perspective Practice**

Tip You can use the Standards Report on **Ed** to check in on students' cumulative proficiency and get helpful resource recommendations.

How will students demonstrate their understanding of the lesson?

Assessment Options

- **Quick Checks** on pages 10 and 14 provide formative assessment to make sure students are understanding the selection.
- **Assessment Practice** on page 15 tests students' overall comprehension of the selection.
- **Analyze the Text** questions on page 16 probe deeper into students' understanding and analysis of the text.
- **Choices** on page 17 provide students with opportunities to apply what they've learned to writing a personal reflection essay, creating a tribute video or illustrated booklet, or conducting a debate.
- **Selection Test** evaluates students' understanding of the selection and skills. You can choose an editable and printable version or an online version that tracks student proficiency on **Ed**.

A Chance in the World   **4B**

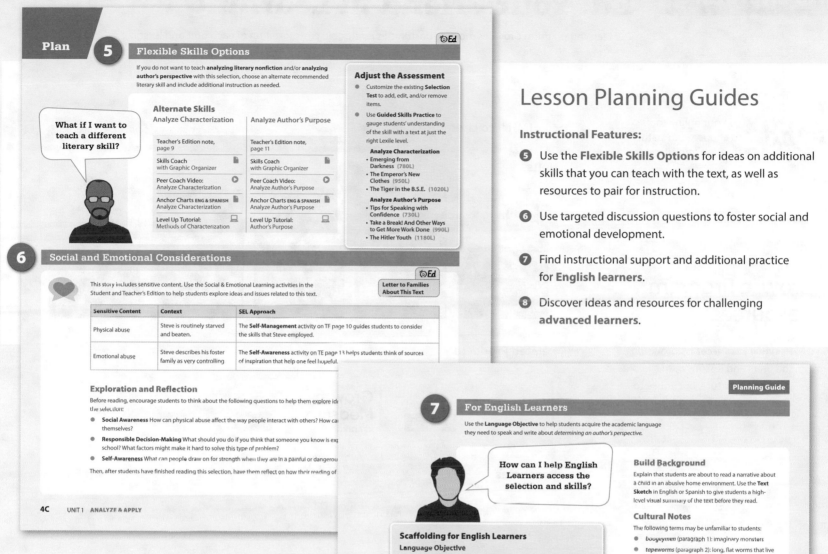

Plan (5)

Flexible Skills Options

If you do not want to teach **analyzing literary nonfiction** and/or **analyzing author's perspective** with this selection, choose an alternate recommended literary skill and include additional instruction as needed.

What if I want to teach a different literary skill?

Alternate Skills

Analyze Characterization	Analyze Author's Purpose
Teacher's Edition note, page 9	Teacher's Edition note, page 11
Skills Coach with Graphic Organizer	Skills Coach with Graphic Organizer
Peer Coach Video: Analyze Characterization	Peer Coach Video: Analyze Author's Purpose
Anchor Charts ENG & SPANISH Analyze Characterization	Anchor Charts ENG & SPANISH Analyze Author's Purpose
Level Up Tutorial: Methods of Characterization	Level Up Tutorial: Author's Purpose

Adjust the Assessment

- Customize the existing **Selection Test** to add, edit, and/or remove items.
- Use **Guided Skills Practice** to gauge students' understanding of the skill with a text at just the right Lexile level.

Analyze Characterization
- Emerging from Darkness (780L)
- The Emperor's New Clothes (950L)
- The Tiger in the B.S.E. (1020L)

Analyze Author's Purpose
- Tips for Speaking with Confidence (730L)
- Take a Break! And Other Ways to Get More Work Done (990L)
- The Hitler Youth (1180L)

(6) ## Social and Emotional Considerations

This story includes sensitive content. Use the Social & Emotional Learning activities in the Student and Teacher's Edition to help students explore ideas and issues related to this text.

Letter to Families About This Text

Sensitive Content	Context	SEL Approach
Physical abuse	Steve is routinely starved and beaten.	The **Self-Management** activity on TE page 10 guides students to consider the skills that Steve employed.
Emotional abuse	Steve describes his foster family as very controlling.	The **Self-Awareness** activity on TE page 13 helps students think of sources of inspiration that help one feel hopeful.

Exploration and Reflection

Before reading, encourage students to think about the following questions to help them explore ide[...] the selection:

- **Social Awareness** How can physical abuse affect the way people interact with others? How ca[...] themselves?
- **Responsible Decision-Making** What should you do if you think that someone you know is exp[...] school? What factors might make it hard to solve this type of problem?
- **Self-Awareness** What can people draw on for strength when they are in a painful or dangerou[...]

Then, after students have finished reading this selection, have them reflect on how their reading of [...]

Lesson Planning Guides

Instructional Features:

(5) Use the **Flexible Skills Options** for ideas on additional skills that you can teach with the text, as well as resources to pair for instruction.

(6) Use targeted discussion questions to foster social and emotional development.

(7) Find instructional support and additional practice for **English learners**.

(8) Discover ideas and resources for challenging **advanced learners**.

Planning Guide

(7) ## For English Learners

Use the **Language Objective** to help students acquire the academic language they need to speak and write about *determining an author's perspective*.

How can I help English Learners access the selection and skills?

Build Background

Explain that students are about to read a narrative about a child in an abusive home environment. Use the **Text Sketch** in English or Spanish to give students a high-level visual summary of the text before they read.

Cultural Notes

The following terms may be unfamiliar to students:

- *boogeymen* (paragraph 1): imaginary monsters
- *tapeworms* (paragraph 2): long, flat worms that live in the intestines of people or animals
- *fair game* (paragraph 4): something permitted according to the rules
- *squirrel it away* (paragraph 4): hide it for future use
- *fit to be eaten* (paragraph 7): suitable to eat
- *take them off their hands* (paragraph 7): relieve them of the burden or responsibility
- *steal down to the cellar* (paragraph 32): go quietly or secretly down to the cellar
- *slings and arrows* (paragraph 32): something unpleasant that is not one's fault
- *sow the seeds* (paragraph 36): start or cause something

Scaffolding for English Learners

Language Objective

Identify language the author uses to establish or reveal his perspective.

Determine Author's Perspective Tell students that an *author's perspective* conveys the author's ideas, values, feelings, or beliefs. Tell students that they will often need to look for evidence in the text that indicates the author's perspective when the author does not state his or her views or beliefs directly.

▶ **Substantial** Think aloud to help students identify words and phrases in the first three paragraphs that help them identify the author's ideas, values, feelings, or beliefs. Then turn to paragraph 4 and help students identify words and phrases that help them determine the author's perspective about the Robinsons.

▶ **Moderate** Display these sentence frames: *The author writes that the Robinsons are _____. This shows he thinks they are _____.* Assist students in finding evidence from the text to help them complete each of these sentence frames.

▶ **Light** Have partners read the **Summary with Targeted Passages** and ask each other questions about how Steve views the Robinsons, Mrs. Levin, his home environment, and the books he reads.

Online Resources

Spanish Resources	Multilingual Glossary
Text Sketch ENG & SPANISH	Summary with Targeted Passages

(8) ## For Students Who Need a Challenge

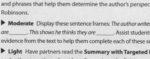

How do I support students who need a challenge?

- **To Challenge Students** notes on pages 8 and 14 provide opportunities for students to extend and enrich their understanding of the text.
- Have students consider how the author writes about his childhood. Have students revisit the personal reflection they wrote on page 17 and explore whether their perspective now differs from their thoughts at the time the event occurred.

A Chance in the World   **4D**

Ed: Your Friend in Learning

Our learning platform provides more opportunities for flexible customization of each unit and lesson.

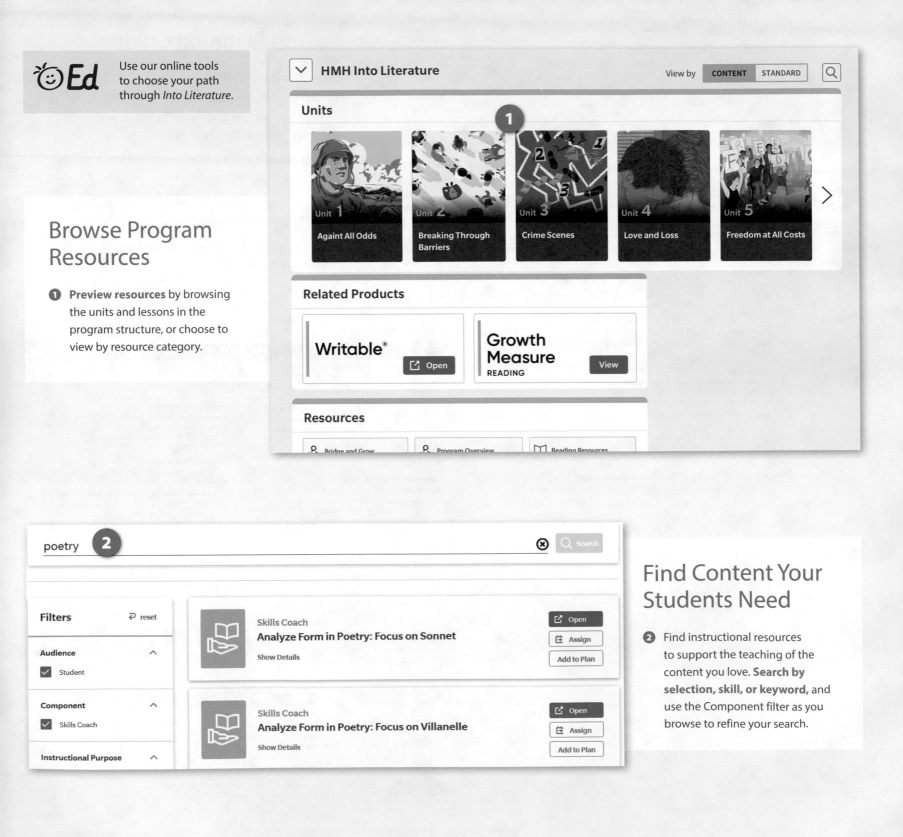

Ed Use our online tools to choose your path through *Into Literature*.

Browse Program Resources

❶ Preview resources by browsing the units and lessons in the program structure, or choose to view by resource category.

HMH Into Literature — View by CONTENT | STANDARD

Units

Unit 1 — Againt All Odds
Unit 2 — Breaking Through Barriers
Unit 3 — Crime Scenes
Unit 4 — Love and Loss
Unit 5 — Freedom at All Costs

Related Products

Writable® — Open
Growth Measure — READING — View

Resources

Bridge and Grow — Program Overview — Reading Resources

Find Content Your Students Need

❷ Find instructional resources to support the teaching of the content you love. **Search by selection, skill, or keyword,** and use the Component filter as you browse to refine your search.

poetry — Search

Filters — reset

Audience
☑ Student

Component
☑ Skills Coach

Instructional Purpose

Skills Coach
Analyze Form in Poetry: Focus on Sonnet
Show Details
Open | Assign | Add to Plan

Skills Coach
Analyze Form in Poetry: Focus on Villanelle
Show Details
Open | Assign | Add to Plan

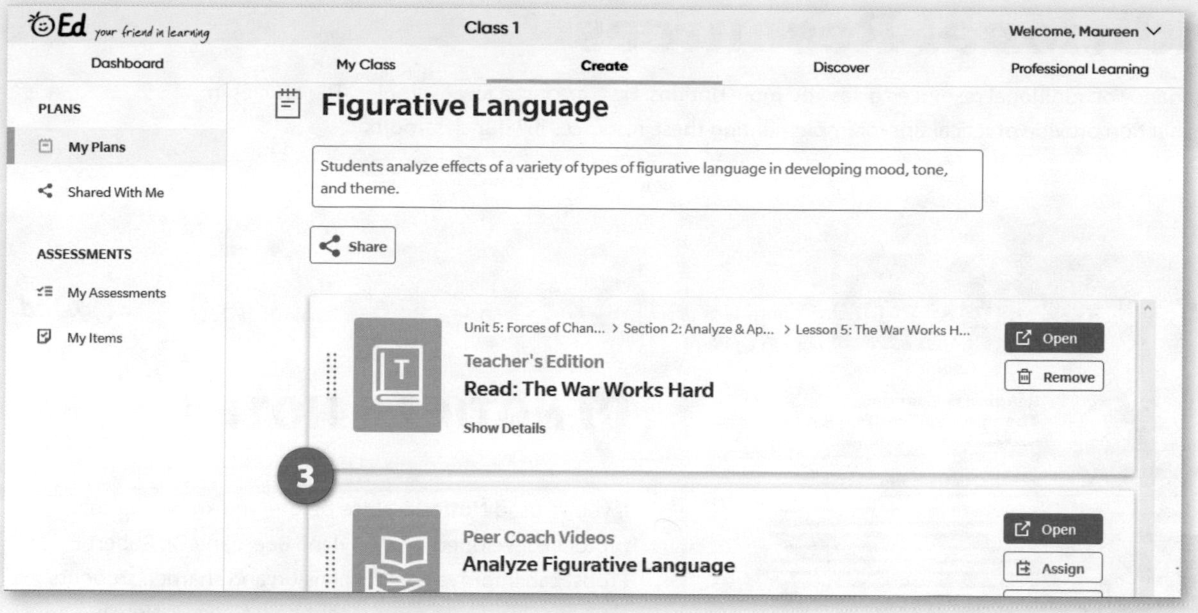

Ed *your friend in learning*

Class 1   Welcome, Maureen ∨

Dashboard   My Class   **Create**   Discover   Professional Learning

PLANS

☐ **My Plans**

≪ Shared With Me

ASSESSMENTS

☑ My Assessments

☑ My Items

🗒 Figurative Language

Students analyze effects of a variety of types of figurative language in developing mood, tone, and theme.

≪ Share

Unit 5: Forces of Chan... > Section 2: Analyze & Ap... > Lesson 5: The War Works H...

[T] Teacher's Edition
Read: The War Works Hard
Show Details

⬈ Open
🗑 Remove

3

Peer Coach Videos
Analyze Figurative Language

⬈ Open
☰ Assign

Create Your Own Lesson Plans

3 **Create your own lesson plans** for each unit. Lessons can become your shortcut to the resources you want to use.

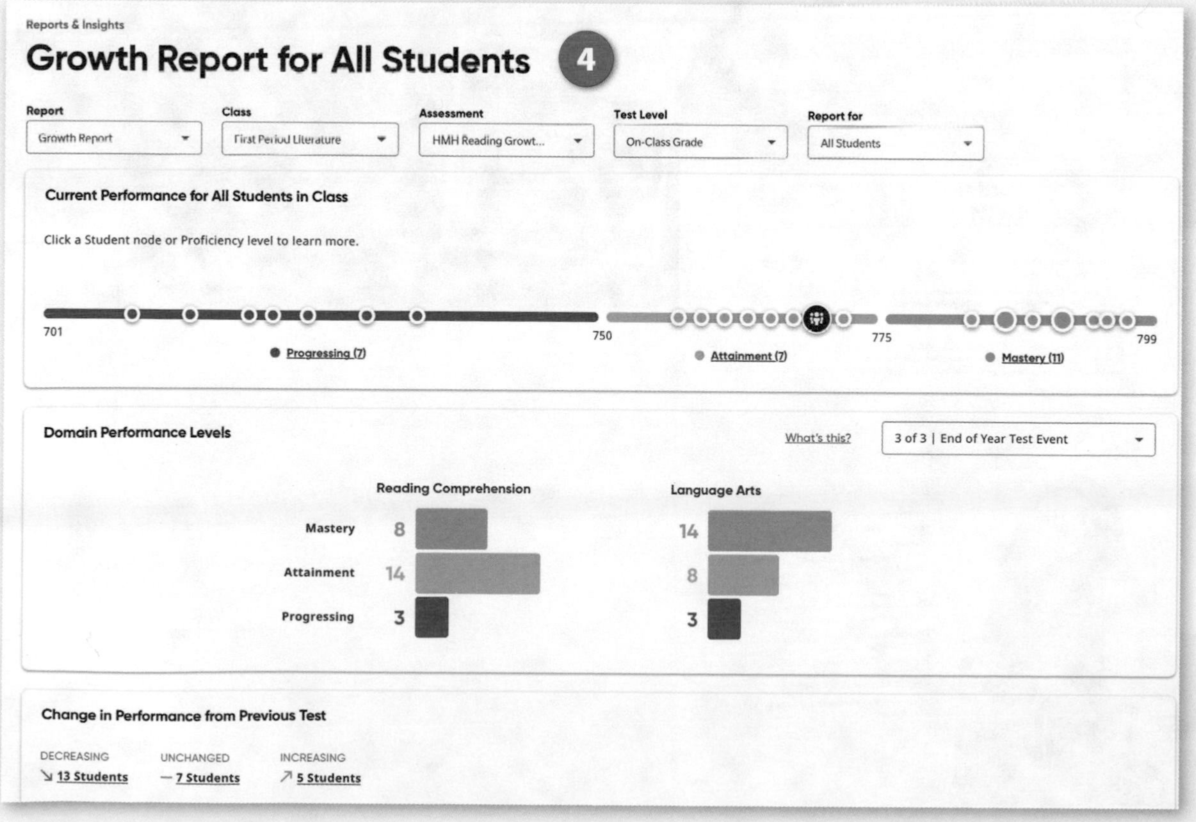

Reports & Insights

Growth Report for All Students **4**

Report	Class	Assessment	Test Level	Report for
Growth Report ▾	First Period Literature ▾	HMH Reading Growt... ▾	On-Class Grade ▾	All Students ▾

Current Performance for All Students in Class

Click a Student node or Proficiency level to learn more.

701   750   775   799

● <u>Progressing (7)</u>   ● <u>Attainment (7)</u>   ● <u>Mastery (11)</u>

Domain Performance Levels

<u>What's this?</u> | 3 of 3 | End of Year Test Event ▾ |

Reading Comprehension

Mastery	8
Attainment	14
Progressing	3

Language Arts

Mastery	14
Attainment	8
Progressing	3

Change in Performance from Previous Test

DECREASING	UNCHANGED	INCREASING
↘ <u>13 Students</u>	— <u>7 Students</u>	↗ <u>5 Students</u>

Differentiate with Data

4 Use the **HMH Growth Measure** or **Standards Report** to drive your planning and differentiation decisions. Learn more on pages 118–119.

Additional Resources

An abundance of additional resources gives you more options. Here are just a few examples. The articles in the next section provide practical tips for implementing these resources in your classroom.

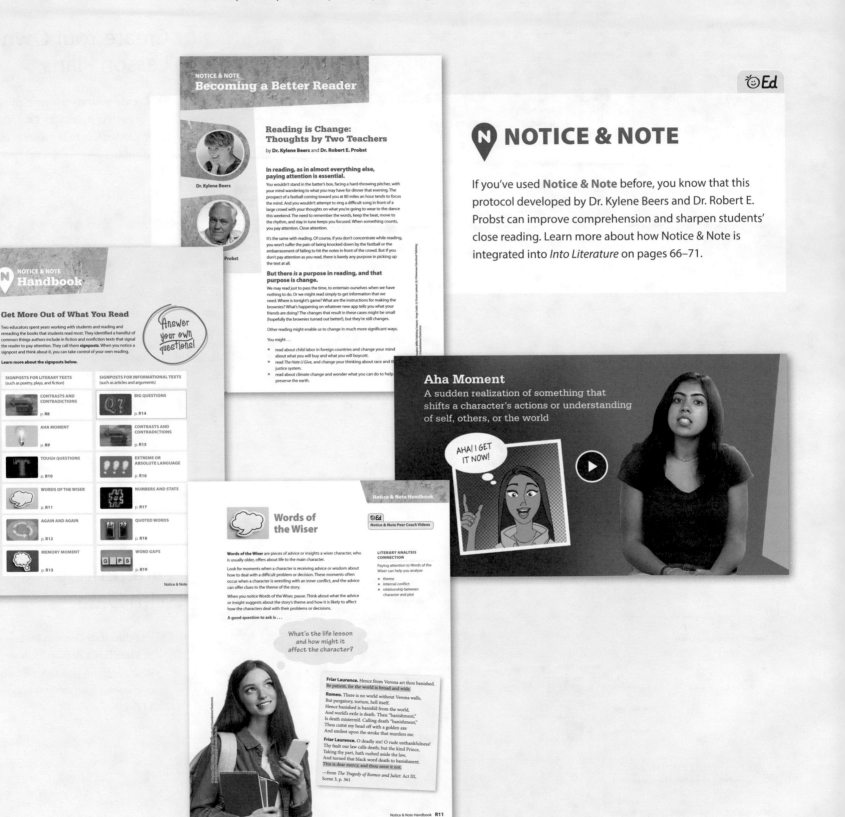

NOTICE & NOTE
Becoming a Better Reader

Reading is Change: Thoughts by Two Teachers
by **Dr. Kylene Beers** and **Dr. Robert E. Probst**

Dr. Kylene Beers

In reading, as in almost everything else, paying attention is essential.

You wouldn't stand in the batter's box, facing a hard-throwing pitcher, with your mind wandering to what you may have for dinner that evening. The prospect of a fastball coming toward you at 80 miles an hour tends to focus the mind. And you wouldn't attempt to sing a difficult song in front of a large crowd with your thoughts on what you're going to wear to the dance this weekend. The need to remember the words, keep the beat, move to the rhythm, and stay in tune keeps you focused. When something counts, you pay attention. Close attention.

It's the same with reading. Of course, if you don't concentrate while reading, you won't suffer the pain of being knocked down by the fastball or the embarrassment of failing to hit the notes in front of the crowd. But if you don't pay attention as you read, there is barely any purpose in picking up the text at all.

But there *is* a purpose in reading, and that purpose is change.

We may read just to pass the time, to entertain ourselves when we have nothing to do. Or we might read simply to get information that we need. Where is tonight's game? What are the instructions for making the brownies? What's happening on whatever new app tells you what your friends are doing? The changes that result in these cases might be small (hopefully the brownies turned out better!), but they're still changes.

Other reading might enable us to change in much more significant ways.

You might . . .

- read about child labor in foreign countries and change your mind about what you will buy and what you will boycott.
- read *The Hate U Give*, and change your thinking about race and the justice system.
- read about climate change and wonder what you can do to help preserve the earth.

NOTICE & NOTE
Handbook

Get More Out of What You Read

Two educators spent years working with students and reading and rereading the books that students read most. They identified a handful of common things authors include in fiction and nonfiction texts that signal the reader to pay attention. They call them **signposts**. When you notice a signpost and think about it, you can take control of your own reading.

Learn more about the signposts below.

Answer your own questions!

SIGNPOSTS FOR LITERARY TEXTS (such as poetry, plays, and fiction)	SIGNPOSTS FOR INFORMATIONAL TEXTS (such as articles and arguments)
CONTRASTS AND CONTRADICTIONS p. R8	BIG QUESTIONS p. R14
AHA MOMENT p. R9	CONTRASTS AND CONTRADICTIONS p. R15
TOUGH QUESTIONS p. R10	EXTREME OR ABSOLUTE LANGUAGE p. R16
WORDS OF THE WISER p. R11	NUMBERS AND STATS p. R17
AGAIN AND AGAIN p. R12	QUOTED WORDS p. R18
MEMORY MOMENT p. R13	WORD GAPS p. R19

Notice & Note

NOTICE & NOTE

If you've used **Notice & Note** before, you know that this protocol developed by Dr. Kylene Beers and Dr. Robert E. Probst can improve comprehension and sharpen students' close reading. Learn more about how Notice & Note is integrated into *Into Literature* on pages 66–71.

Aha Moment
A sudden realization of something that shifts a character's actions or understanding of self, others, or the world

AHA! I GET IT NOW!

Notice & Note Handbook

Words of the Wiser

Notice & Note Peer Coach Videos

Words of the Wiser are pieces of advice or insights a wiser character, who is usually older, offers about life to the main character.

Look for moments when a character is receiving advice or wisdom about how to deal with a difficult problem or decision. These moments often occur when a character is wrestling with an inner conflict, and the advice can offer clues to the theme of the story.

When you notice Words of the Wiser, pause. Think about what the advice or insight suggests about the story's theme and how it is likely to affect how the characters deal with their problems or decisions.

A good question to ask is . . .

What's the life lesson and how might it affect the character?

LITERARY ANALYSIS CONNECTION

Paying attention to Words of the Wiser can help you analyze

- theme
- internal conflict
- relationship between character and plot

Friar Laurence. Hence from Verona art thou banished.
Be patient, for the world is broad and wide.
Romeo. There is no world without Verona walls,
But purgatory, torture, hell itself.
Hence banished is banish'd from the world,
And world's exile is death. Then "banishment,"
Is death mistermid. Calling death "banishment,"
Thou cutts't my head off with a golden axe
And smilest upon the stroke that murders me.
Friar Laurence. O deadly sin! O rude unthankfulness!
Thy fault our law calls death; but the kind Prince,
Taking thy part, hath rushed aside the law,
And turned that black word death to banishment.
This is dear mercy, and thou seest it not.

—from *The Tragedy of Romeo and Juliet:* Act III, Scene 3, p. 361

Notice & Note Handbook **R11**

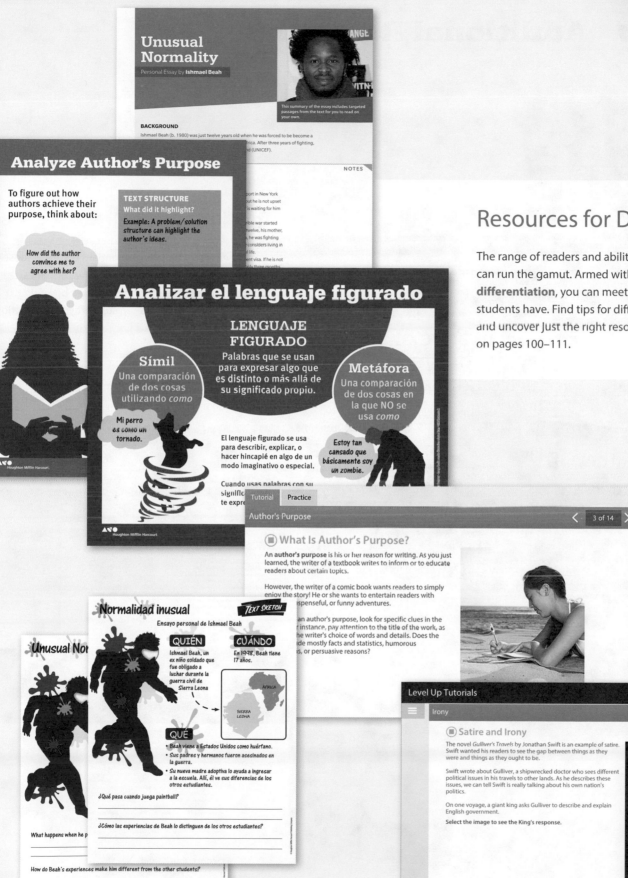

Resources for Differentiation

The range of readers and abilities in your classroom can run the gamut. Armed with the right resources for **differentiation**, you can meet the many needs your students have. Find tips for differentiating instruction and uncover just the right resources to do that effectively on pages 100–111.

Additional Resources

STUDY GUIDE

I Know Why the Caged Bird Sings
by Maya Angelou

TEACHER NOTES
- Background
- Pacing Guide
- Social and Emotional C...

STUDY GUIDE
- Student Anticipation Gu...
- Vocabulary Tracker
- Read and Respond with...

ASSESSMENTS
- Writing Prompts
- Creative Projects
- Book Test (Multiple Cho...
  Go online to assign this book test.

ANSWER KEY

Houghton Mifflin Harcourt.

STUDY GUIDE

In the Time of the Butterflies
by Julia Alvarez

TEACHER NOTES
- Background
- Pacing Guide
- Social and Emotio...

STUDY GUIDE
- Student Anticipat...
- Vocabulary Tracke...
- Read and Respon...

ASSESSMENTS
- Writing Prompts
- Creative Projects

Houghton Mifflin Harcourt.

HMH DIGITAL LIBRARY

Narrative of the Life of Frederick Douglass

Frederick Douglass

HMH DIGITAL L...

Wuthering H...

Emily Brontë

HMH DIGI...

Poetry an...

Edgar Allan Poe

Social Media: More Good Than Harm
Argument by Timothy Brewer

For most of us, social media is a big part of our lives. Apps such as Facebook, Instagram, Snapchat, and Twitter are how most of us communicate, share news, and express ourselves. Some people say that social media is bad for society and the individual. They feel that these platforms are too distracting and prevent people from really thinking. However, when you consider the benefits of social media, it's easy to see that these apps do more good than harm.

First, consider that social media exposes us to a wide variety of perspectives and people we might not ever see otherwise. For example, just by opening Instagram on your phone you can see what life is like in Bangladesh. You can learn what people are protesting about in South America. You can see what movements are trending by clicking various hashtags. On Facebook or Twitter, you can interact and converse with someone who holds totally different views from yours and gain a better t...

Good Gaming!
Argument by Hillary Brown

Oscar Wilde once said, "Everything in moderation, including moderation." Though this applies to many things in life, it is particularly relevant to gaming. In today's world, people have many different views about the usefulness and perceived negative effects of videogames. Often people view videogames as a waste of time, and some have even argued that the violence in videogames causes people to also become more violent. However, the research on these points of view is varied, with inconclusive results. Meanwhile, the gaming industry has only picked up speed. While it is true that playing nonstop may have negative effects like diminishing our time spent exercising and socializing, gaming also has great potential benefits. Some examples of these are that games can help students obtain scholarships, provide a platform for kids to practice perseverance, and relieve the negative effects of stress, depression, and more.

Scholarship Bound

Understandably, previous generations may not understand

Text Library

Flexibility starts with having abundant texts to choose from, including novels, ripped-from-the-headlines nonfiction connections, and more. Learn how *Into Literature's* **library of texts** can support your instructional goals on pages 44–47.

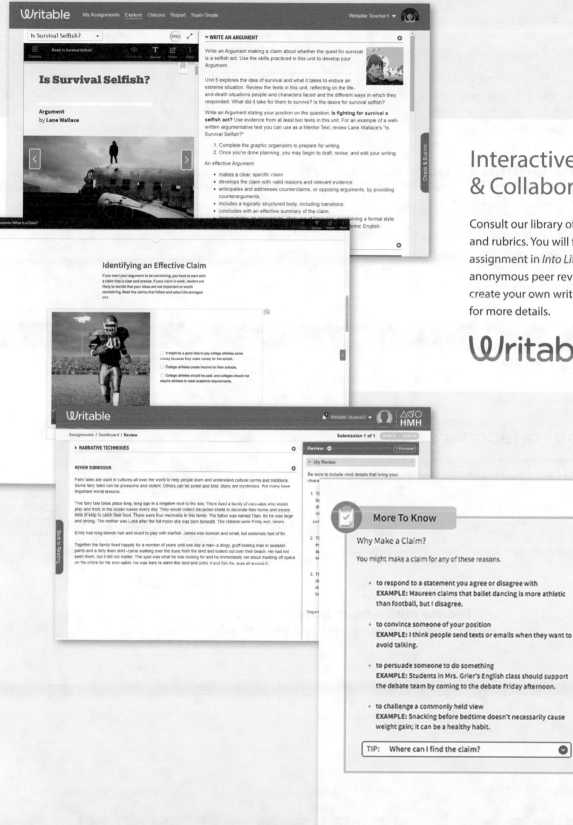

Interactive Writing & Collaboration

Consult our library of prompts, instructional supports, and rubrics. You will find digital support for each writing assignment in *Into Literature*. Use **Writable** to facilitate anonymous peer reviews, get help grading essays, or create your own writing assignments. See pages 78 83 for more details.

Writable

Teacher's Corner

We want you to feel confident teaching with *Into Literature*—and that comes with ongoing support. In addition to your initial implementation of professional learning, **Teacher's Corner** gives you the support you want with an ever-growing library of bite-size professional learning resources, from authentic class videos to tips from others teacher and our team of experienced coaches.

So whether you want to quickly prep for a lesson or invest time in your professional growth, we have trusted resources to enhance your instruction and class tomorrow.

On-Demand, But Not One-Size-Fits-All

We put the professional learning in your hands—choose the pace and time to get the support you need. Browse resources aligned to your programs and beyond to get started, pick up implementation tips, and stay inspired with lesson ideas and new research.

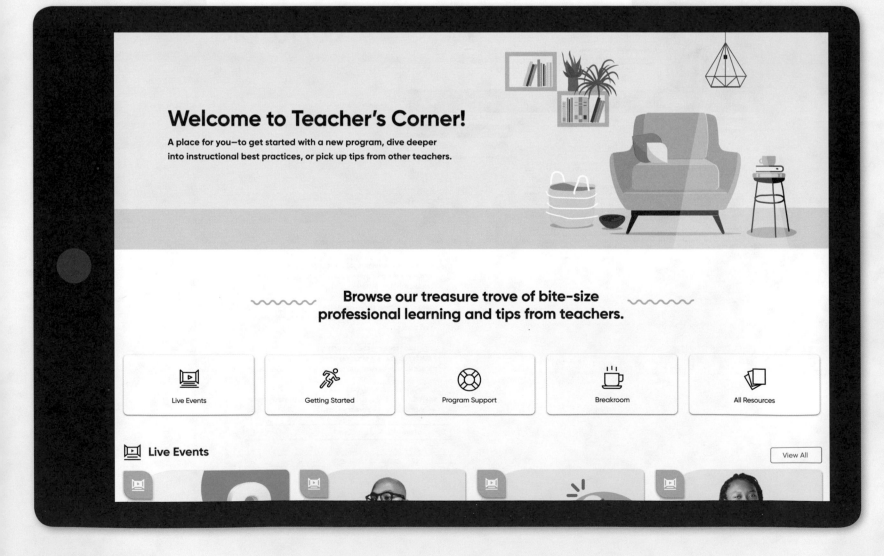

Welcome to Teacher's Corner!

A place for you—to get started with a new program, dive deeper into instructional best practices, or pick up tips from other teachers.

Browse our treasure trove of bite-size professional learning and tips from teachers.

| Live Events | Getting Started | Program Support | Breakroom | All Resources |

Live Events   View All

Curated, Trusted Content

There's no shortage of free resources online, but with Teacher's Corner, professional learning and instructional recommendations align to best practices. Hear exclusively from prominent thought leaders, experienced coaches, and practicing teachers.

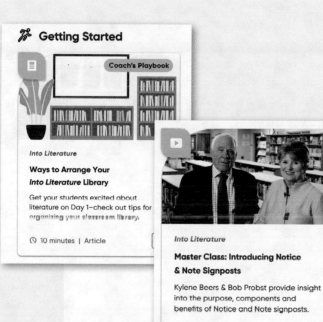

Ready & Relevant for Tomorrow's Instruction

Designed to be practical and applicable to planning and teaching, Teacher's Corner includes authentic class videos, expert videos, interactive articles, and podcasts.

A Community of Live Support

Our Live Events give you exclusive access to extend your learning by connecting with our instructional coaches, thought leaders, and each other.

Flexibility & Choice

40   Planning the Year

44   Adapting Units of Instruction

48   Teaching with Novels and Longer Works

Planning the Year

Getting to Know *Into Literature*

Explore Six Thematic Units

With its deliberate instructional design, *Into Literature* moves students from guided whole-class instruction to small-group peer collaboration to independence. Here is an overview of the key features in each unit.

Unit Opener

- 2–3 engagement activities to help students connect to the unit theme

Analyze & Apply

- 2–4 lessons, each with an accompanying **Selection Test**
- 1–2 **Mentor Texts**, authentic examples of the type of writing students will do at the end of the unit

Collaborate & Compare

- 1–2 text groupings so students can think critically across related texts, with an accompanying **Selection Test**

Reader's Choice

- 4–6 short read recommendations for independent reading with an accompanying **Selection Test**

- 3 long read recommendations for independent reading, with an accompanying **Book Test**

End-of-Unit Tasks

- 1 writing assignment
- 1 speaking & listening assignment
- 1 media project
- 1 **Unit Test**

> **What have you given me to work with?**

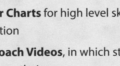
Ed

Additional Support

Text Library

- Texts across different genres and Lexile® ranges
- Digital novels and nonfiction texts
- Printable **Reader's Choice** texts
- HMH Study Guides and assessments

Text Support

- **Adapted Texts and Summaries**, and **Text Sketch** overviews to support struggling readers and English learners
- **Notice & Note Anchor Charts** to support close reading
- **Multilingual Glossaries**, with terms in 10 languages
- **Spanish Unit Resources**
- **Close Read Screencasts and Practice** to model what close reading sounds like

Skills Support

- **Anchor Charts** for high level skills instruction
- **Peer Coach Videos**, in which students can learn from their peers
- **Guided Skills Practice**, providing targeted skills practice paired with texts at a range of Lexile® levels for just the right fit
- **Level Up Tutorials and Practice Tests** for independent practice and remediation
- **Interactive Writing**, **Grammar**, **Vocabulary**, and **Speaking & Listening Lessons** for additional practice
- **Media Projects** connected to each unit theme

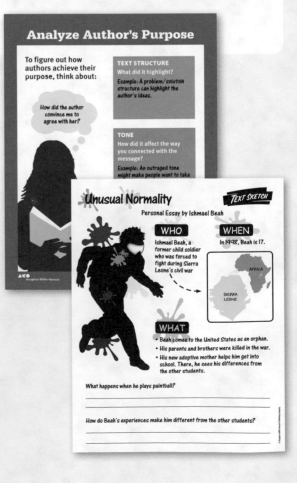

Analyze Author's Purpose

To figure out how authors achieve their purpose, think about:

How did the author convince me to agree with her?

TEXT STRUCTURE
What did it highlight?
Example: A problem/solution structure can highlight the author's ideas.

TONE
How did it affect the way you connected with the message?
Example: An outraged tone might make people want to take

Unusual Normality
TEXT SKETCH

Personal Essay by Ishmael Beah

WHO
Ishmael Beah, a former child soldier who was forced to fight during Sierra Leone's civil war

WHEN
In 1998, Beah is 17.

AFRICA
SIERRA LEONE

WHAT
- Beah comes to the United States as an orphan.
- His parents and brothers were killed in the war.
- His new adoptive mother helps him get into school. There, he sees his differences from the other students.

What happens when he plays paintball?

_____

How do Beah's experiences make him different from the other students?

_____

Getting to Know *Into Literature*

Pick and Choose

Into Literature includes more than 180 days of instruction, which means you have plenty of options. Where you choose to spend time and what you choose to set aside will affect your overall pacing, but we've provided supports in the Teacher's Edition to help you make these decisions.

Can I really do all of this in one year?

- Use the pacing recommendations for each Unit Opener so you can gauge about how much time it will take to introduce a unit. Spend additional time on background and engagement activities or skip them entirely.

- Consult the **Lesson Planning Guide** for each text to find realistic pacing suggestions for pre-teaching, reading, and post-reading activities and instruction. Consider these a starting point for pacing, as you think through how much you can cover within the academic year.

📅 1 INTRODUCE THE UNIT: 1 day

Set the Stage

▶ Introduce the unit by playing the **Stream to Start** video.

📅 6 Suggested Pacing: 6 Days (50 minute classes)

Get Ready: 1 Day   **Read:** 3 Days   **Respond:** 2 Days

Day 1: paragraphs 1–77 | **Day 2:** paragraphs 78–246 | **Day 3:** paragraphs 247–278

- **Ed** If you follow a benchmark of nine weeks per unit, you might choose to include only four of the six units. You can easily piece together "gap lessons" to address any additional standards or skills by using our **Anchor Charts**, **Peer Coach Videos**, and **Skills Coach** resources, all available on our learning platform.

- Another factor that will affect your pacing is how much class time students will spend working through readings and assignments. Should you decide to do much of the reading in class, instead of assigning it as homework, you'll need to build in more time. The same would apply for the end-of-unit writing task—if you prefer to have students completing this assignment in class, this will require additional time.

📅 5 Suggested Pacing: 5 Days (50 minute classes)

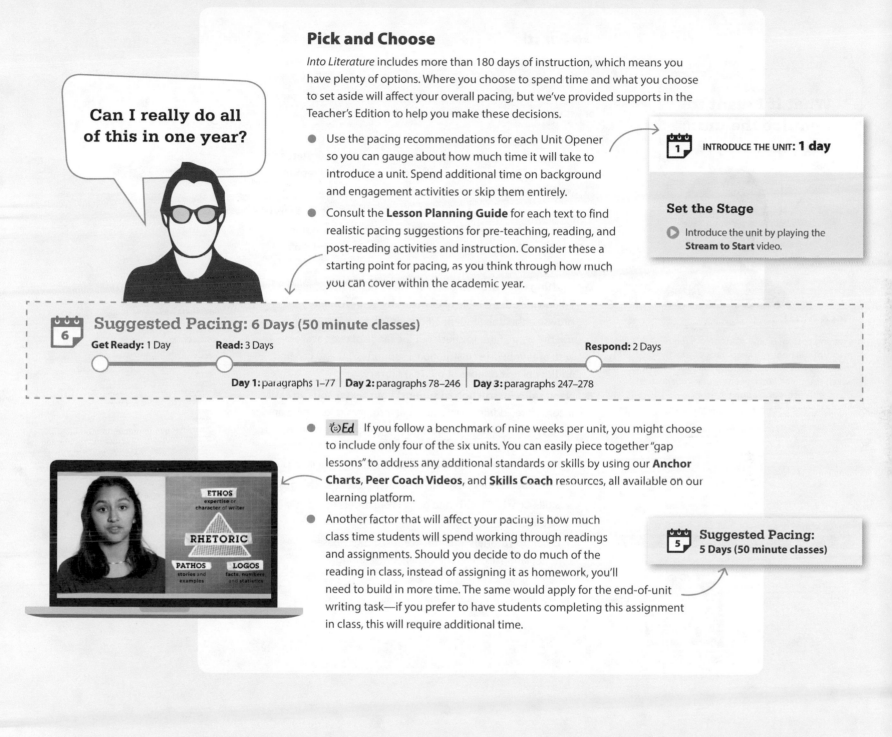

What if I want to organize the units in other ways?

Tips & Tricks!

Creating custom digital plans on our learning platform will help you keep track of exactly the resources you want to use, and manage who gets which resources. You can also share your custom plans with peers and administrators.

Go For It!

We have organized our units thematically, but *Into Literature* is flexible enough to support what you need, whether your district plans and delivers curriculum to you, or you are building it yourself or with a team.

● **Building units around standards?** No problem. You can use our learning platform to browse content by your state's standards. Then use filters to hone in on the kind of resources you're looking for.

● **Incorporating novels into your curriculum?** That works too. Consult the suggested long reads connected to each unit, as well as the accompanying **HMH Study Guide** and digital assessment online.

● **Crafting units around genres?** You've got it. The Student Edition includes a Table of Contents by genre. Online, you can browse either the Student Edition or Teacher's Edition and use the genre filter to check out the range of texts available with our embedded instructional supports. You also can find additional text options in the **Text Library**.

● **Need skills instruction to support your texts?** You can easily incorporate additional instructional resources to pair with any texts you've added. The following resources are waiting for you on the platform:

  • **Anchor Charts:** High-level visual summaries of skills and ideas

  • **Peer Coach Videos:** Videos of students' peers teaching skills

  • **Skills Coach:** Skills-based graphic organizers that can be paired with any text

  • **Level Up Tutorials and Practice Tests:** Skills-based remediation lessons for independent learning

Teaching the Standards

> **How can I make sure I have covered all of my state's standards?**

We've Got You

Consult these program resources as you formulate your instructional plans at the beginning of the year.

- **⊙Ed** Find the lesson that you want to teach on Ed. Each text is tagged to your state standards.

- You can also refer to the **Unit Planning Guides** in the Teacher's Edition and at the end of this Program Guide to see the skills coverage for each unit. See pages 146–169.

- **⊙Ed** As the year progresses and you want to teach a specific standard, use the Filter by Standards on Ed to find a text.

- **⊙Ed** Pair our online **Skills Coach** resources with texts you're trying to teach to meet tricky-to-cover standards.

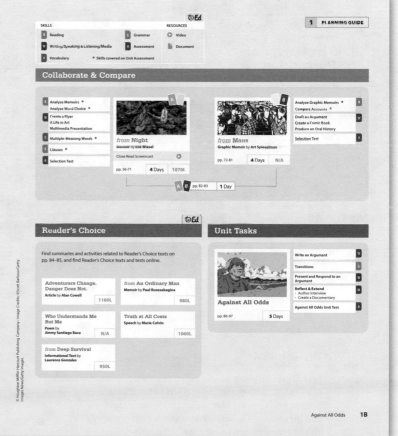

UNIT 1

PLANNING GUIDE

Against All Odds

ESSENTIAL QUESTION: What does it take to survive a crisis?

SKILLS

R Reading
W Writing/Speaking/Listening/Media
V Vocabulary
G Grammar
A Assessment

* Skills covered on Unit Assessment

RESOURCES

Video
Document

1 PLANNING GUIDE

Analyze & Apply

from A Chance in the World
Literary Nonfiction by Steve Pemberton
Text Sketch ENG & SPANISH
Summary with Targeted Passages
pp. 4–19 | 5 Days | 1070L

- Analyze Literary Nonfiction * R
- Analyze Author's Perspective * R
- Personal Reflection W
- Debate
- Tribute
- Patterns of Word Changes * V
- Colons and Semicolons * G
- Selection Test A

Is Survival Selfish?
MENTOR TEXT
Argument by Lane Wallace
Text Sketch ENG & SPANISH
Summary with Targeted Passages
pp. 20–21 | 4 Days | 1000L

- Analyze Arguments * R
- Analyze Rhetorical Devices * R
- Selfish or Smart? W
- Group Discussion
- Survivor Tales
- Synonyms * V
- Commas * G
- Selection Test A

The Leap
Short Story by Louis Erdrich
Text Sketch ENG & SPANISH
Summary with Targeted Passages
pp. 32–47 | 4 Days | 1070L

- Analyze Flashback and Tension * R
- Make Inferences * R
- Retell the Story W
- Group Discussion
- Build a Timeline
- Prefixes * V
- Relative Clauses * G
- Selection Test A

The End and the Beginning
Poem by Wisława Szymborska
pp. 48–55 | 4 Days | N/A

- Analyze Poetic Language * R
- Analyze Poetic Structure *3 R
- Write a Dialogue W
- Podcast
- Blog
- Selection Test A

Collaborate & Compare

- Analyze Memoirs * R
- Analyze Word Choice * R
- Create a Flyer W
- A Life in Art
- Multimedia Presentation
- Multiple-Meaning Words * V
- Clauses * G
- Selection Test A

from Night
Memoir by Elie Wiesel
Close Read Screencast
pp. 56–71 | 4 Days | 1070L

- Analyze Graphic Memoirs * R
- Compare Accounts * R
- Draft an Argument W
- Create a Comic Book
- Produce an Oral History
- Selection Test A

from Maus
Graphic Memoir by Art Spiegelman
pp. 72–81 | 4 Days | N/A

A B pp. 82–83 | 1 Day

Reader's Choice

⊙Ed

Find summaries and activities related to Reader's Choice texts on pp. 84–85, and find Reader's Choice texts and tests online.

Adventurers Change. Danger Does Not.
Article by Alan Cowell
1160L

from An Ordinary Man
Memoir by Paul Rusesabagina
980L

Who Understands Me But Me
Poem by Jimmy Santiago Baca
N/A

Truth at All Costs
Speech by Marie Colvin
1060L

from Deep Survival
Informational Text by Laurence Gonzales
950L

Unit Tasks

Against All Odds
pp. 86–97 | 5 Days

- Write an Argument W
- Transitions
- Present and Respond to an Argument W
- Reflect & Extend W
  - Author Interview
  - Create a Documentary
- Against All Odds Unit Test A

© Houghton Mifflin Harcourt Publishing Company • Image Credits: (t) ©Jan H Andersen/Shutterstock; (b) ©Cavan Images/Getty Images; (bl) ©Ozgy Massey/The Image Bank/Getty Images; (br) ©Wissam Al-Okaili/AFP/Getty Images

© Houghton Mifflin Harcourt Publishing Company • Image Credits: ©Scott Barbour/Getty Images News/Getty Images

Adapting Units of Instruction

Using the Planning Guides

What's the most practical and efficient way to plan a unit?

Start with Your Learning Goals

Whether you are working with a curriculum map, pacing requirements, or other guidelines prescribed by your district, or are at liberty to develop your own curriculum, *Into Literature* has the resources you need to make effective teaching decisions.

● With your learning goals in mind, survey the standards included on the **Unit Planning Guide** and preview the cumulative activities on the **End-of-Unit Tasks Planning Guide.** Determine how you will assess student mastery: with a writing assignment, a project, a summative assessment, or a combination. Choose what to include in the unit based on what students will need to know to demonstrate mastery in these tasks.

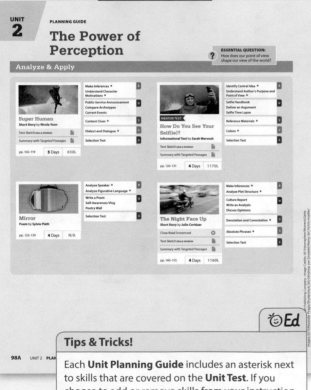

Tips & Tricks!

Each **Unit Planning Guide** includes an asterisk next to skills that are covered on the **Unit Test**. If you choose to add or remove skills from your instruction, you may want to adjust the assessment accordingly. You can do this by editing the Word document and printing it out or using the custom assessment features on Ed and assigning the test digitally.

● Look closely at the **Unit Planning Guide** to get a sense of the texts, authors, genres, skills/standards, and suggested pacing for that unit.

● Preview the **Reader's Choice** options, including the Short Reads and Long Reads. Consider how you will incorporate independent reading in this unit. Think about additional titles you might like to recommend.

Using the Planning Guides

Plan for What You Need

Into Literature provides a number of pacing guidelines to help you plan.

- Begin by reviewing the suggested pacing in the **Unit Planning Guide**. These are realistic estimates of how much time a lesson might take, but you are the best judge of the pacing for your students.

- There is more in-depth guidance on pacing in the **Lesson Planning Guide** pages, so spend a few minutes scanning each of the lessons.

What's the average time for teaching a unit?

The Book of the Dead
Short Story by Edwidge Dantica

Text Sketch ENG & SPANISH

Summary with Targeted Passages

pp. 4–23 | **5** Days | 920L

Analyze Development of Theme *	R
Understand Cultural and Historical Context *	
Write a Letter Visual Art Haitian History	W
Oxymoron *	V
Noun Phrases and Verb Phrases *	G
Selection Test	A

Plan

The Book of the Dead

Short Story by **Edwidge Danticat,** pp. 4–23

Lesson Overview

5 **Suggested Pacing: 5 Days (50-minute classes)**

Get Ready: 1 Day   **Read:** 2 Days   **Respond:** 2 Days

Day 1: paragraphs 1–60 | **Day 2:** paragraphs 61–142

- As you teach the lesson, look for embedded reminders of the pacing along the way, and a Quick Check formative assessment at the end of each day so you can monitor your students' understanding as you progress through the text.

2 WHOLE-CLASS READING: **2 days**

Quick Check

Pacing
Paragraphs 1–60   DAY 1

Use this quick Group Wipeout activity to check students' understanding of the story so far. Pose the first question and have groups discuss it. The first group to hold up the correct answer on their whiteboard wins a point for the group. Repeat with [the other quest]ions.

- [Why does the na]rrator need to speak with the [... a]nd the police officer?

- Why does the narrator's sculpture show her father crouched with his head down?

- Why does Gabrielle Fonteneau want to give the sculpture to her own father?

What If My Students Don't Get It?

IF all groups are not able to answer the questions, **THEN** reread aloud passages that contain the answers (paragraphs 1, 20, 54).

Make the Unit Work for You

There are many adjustments you can make to each unit, and there are tips in the **Unit Planning Guide** to help you along.

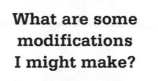

What are some modifications I might make?

- Omit or swap out texts, based on student interest, time, or level of difficulty.

- "Upgrade" **Reader's Choice** selections as texts with instruction.

- Add your own texts or lessons into the mix, especially if you have personal favorites that match the theme or topic of the unit.

- Use a novel or Long Read as the anchor for a particular unit, supplementing it with the texts in the Student Edition.

- Change the skills/standards focus of a particular text, or cover even more skills and standards with the texts you are teaching. In many cases, the **Lesson Planning Guide** includes suggested alternate skills you might use.

- Choose a specific type of writing, media, or speaking and listening end-of-unit task, depending on what your students need more practice in or in preparation for a high-stakes assessment.

- *Ed* Give students more opportunities to apply key skills in the unit to fresh reads. You can do this by
  - choosing one of the Short Read or Long Read options suggested in the **Unit Planning Guide.**
  - visiting the **Text Library** on Ed and filtering by Lexile® or genre.
  - entering the skill as a search term on the platform and then using the component filter to select the **Leveled Text Library.**

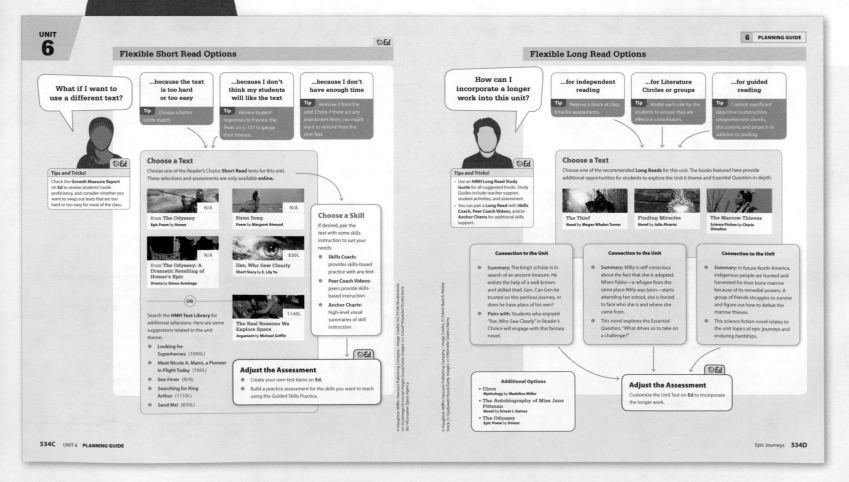

Customizing the Unit

What resources do you have that will help me make these changes?

Tips & Tricks!

For platform power users, you might consider using the available customization tools:
- Create custom lesson plans and build exactly the instruction you need.
- Start with *Into Literature* assessments. Edit them to suit your needs, adding your own items.

Featured Resource: Guided Skills Practice

Guided Skills Practice provides practice opportunities tied to particular skills. Each practice includes a leveled passage and a few related test items. A range of passages is available for each skill, so you can provide students with practice on that skill with a reading that is at *just* the right Lexile® level. For example:

Evaluate Author's Argument

- Some devices recognize your face. Is that a good thing? 700L
- Send Me! 800L
- Risk and Exploration Revisited 900L
- What Teenagers Need to Thrive 1000L
- Life in the Treetops 1100L

Find Flexible Options

Find the resources you need to meet your learning goals.

If you want to...	Try This!	Where?
Find different texts to include in the unit...	● Leveled Texts across genres and at just the right Lexile® level ● Printable Reader's Choice texts	**Text Library**
Incorporate a novel or other longer work...	● Digital novels and nonfiction texts ● HMH Study Guides and companion assessments	**Text Library**
Teach skills different from, or in addition to, those provided in the Student Edition...	● Anchor Charts ● Peer Coach Videos ● Guided Skills Practice ● Level Up Tutorials and Practice Tests ● Skills Coach	**Intervention, Review, & Extension**
Provide extra practice opportunities for covered skills...	● Interactive Writing, Grammar, Vocabulary, and Speaking & Listening Lessons ● Guided Skills Practice ● Level Up Tutorials and Practice Tests ● Skills Coach	● **Writing Resources** ● **Grammar Resources** ● **Vocabulary Resources** ● **Speaking & Listening Resources** ● **Intervention, Review, & Extension**
Use different cumulative tasks...	● End-of-Unit Tasks and Reflect & Extend ● Interactive Writing Lessons ● Interactive Media Projects	● **Teacher's Edition** ● **Writing Resources** ● **Media Projects**

⊠ Full Screen   1 of 3   ⊕ Accessibility

Passage 1

Read the text and choose the best answer to each question.

Send Me!

Blog by Aarini Agate

(1)When I was a kid, I had this recurring dream. I would look down at two feet wrapped in thick, padded boots. The boots bounced carrying my featherweight body, half-floating across a strange, silent, land. I'd wake with a start, thinking how strange to dream of feet. Blinking, a flash of joy rose in me at the realization—I was walking on the surface of Mars!

(2)That's crazy, right? Well, I still have that dream. Only it has become my goal in real life. I want to be one of the first people to live on the planet Mars. To some, that is truly outrageous! Skeptics ask, "Why do you want to die on Mars?" I ask, "Why do you want to die on Earth?" That may sound harsh, but an explorer has to be willing to take a different perspective.

(3)When early European settlers set sail for the New World, they said good-bye to their families, and most never returned. Most had no expectation of seeing their loved ones again. They risked the journey because they wanted to make a fresh start, to begin again, to

Select the phrase where the author first introduces an argument.

Becoming an astronaut requires decades of education, research, and training, with no guarantee of boarding a spaceship. I learned about a group of scientists and engineers who plan to send the first humans to Mars in just a few years. Their company is called Mars Now. Here's the best part—they're seeking volunteers, and anyone can apply. Applicants must be 18. At age 13, I'm ineligible, but I believe I am a strong candidate. In five years, I hope they will be ready for me!

Check Answer

Teaching with Novels and Longer Works

Understanding the Options

How do novels fit into the *Into Literature* course of study?

☺*Ed*

Tips & Tricks!

Find eBooks of classic novels in the **Digital Library** on Ed. These can be assigned to all your students.

The Decision Is Up to You and Your Department

Whether you are looking for novels and other long reads that complement unit themes and skills or planning to incorporate titles you already teach regularly, *Into Literature* can support your practice. Take time to check out the resources that are available.

- Preview the **Suggested Long Reads** for each unit. The **Flexible Long Read Options** page in the Unit Planning Guide is the place to start. You'll find information about the three recommended titles that are featured in the Student Edition and supported with robust **Study Guides**, as well as about two additional recommended titles supported by a modified Study Guide. All Study Guides can be found online.

- Familiarize yourself with the **Study Guides**. They include teacher notes, a vocabulary tracker, analysis questions, writing prompts, assessments, and other support for previewing the book and teaching it in a variety of ways.

- ☺*Ed* Gather support for any additional titles you want to bring in. This might include **Peer Coach** and **Skills Coach** for the reinforcement of relevant skills, **Notice & Note writing frames** and **bookmarks**, and **interactive graphic organizers**.

- Make some choices. Each unit includes more texts than you can cover in a six- or eight-week course of study, especially when factoring in the suggested Long Reads and Reader's Choice selections. You have to decide what to use, and how. Will you teach a novel as a whole-class project, offer several novels to choose from for Literature Circles, assign students independent reading, or some combination throughout the year?

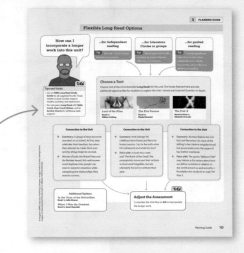

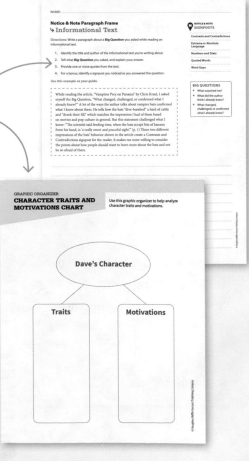

Choosing Your Approach

How can I implement a successful whole-class long read?

Ⓞ Ed

Tips & Tricks!

The **Notice & Note Chart** on pages T28–T30 of the Teacher's Edition includes examples of each signpost drawn from recommended long read titles. If you expect students to use signposts, consider using one of these examples to model how.

Create an Experience That Brings the Class Together

Whole-class reads allow you to create exposure to important books and model best practices for analyzing long works. Many teachers assign a whole-class read in the first part of the school year and then allow students more choice in later grading periods. Others may only have time to teach one novel a year and choose a whole-class experience that everyone can share.

Since so many students will be spending so much time on it, take care to choose a worthy title with wide appeal. The Teacher's Notes in the **Study Guide** can help you.

- Read about the author and, where relevant, critical perspectives.

- Preview key themes and literary elements.

- Scan the **Social and Emotional Considerations** section in the Teacher's Notes, which can help you anticipate whether a book is likely to meet your community's standards and whether you may want to communicate with parents and guardians before reading.

Sensitive Content	Context	Evaluating the Outcome
War	The book takes place during a fictional atomic war. A paratrooper killed in the fighting is misinterpreted by the boys as the "beast" and gradually decomposes.	The wartime setting is crucial to the development of the plot. **Ask:** How might the author's experience in World War II have influenced his ideas about human nature? How are those ideas expressed in the novel?
Bullying	Piggy is bullied by the other boys for being overweight, unathletic, and near-sighted.	Unlike most of the other boys, Piggy is conscientious and strategic. **Ask:** How does Piggy respond to bullying? How does Ralph's treatment of Piggy change?
Missing child who is presumed dead	After the boys accidentally set fire to a section of the forest, a young boy is unaccounted for.	Piggy worries about what happened to the boy. **Ask:** How do the older children treat the younger children? What theme might their behavior suggest?
Murder of Simon	The boys mistake Simon for the beast and, in a frenzied "dance," beat him to death.	The event marks the boys' descent into savagery. The boys recast the experience, avoiding the truth. **Ask:** How can the actions of a group seem to erase individual accountability?
Murder of Piggy	Sadistic Roger hurls a rock off the cliff at Piggy. Piggy falls to his death.	Piggy's death strikes a final blow against Ralph's attempts to keep order. **Ask:** How does Ralph feel after Piggy dies? What does he realize about Piggy?

How do I make Literature Circles work in my classroom?

Allow Choice and Set Expectations

Many teachers find that allowing students some choice increases their motivation and focus. Literature Circles or book groups are a good way to do this, as long as you provide enough structure.

- Use the **Suggested Long Reads** and/or other books available to you to create a list for students to choose from. Ask students to pick a first and second choice so that you have some options for balancing groups. As much as possible, form groups based on book choice, not ability.

- Assign students jobs that cater to their specific skills, drawn from the roles shown below. Allow students to switch roles as they wish, emphasizing student choice.

Leader

Note Taker

Time Keeper

Participation Tracker

- Tell group members to develop a reading schedule. They should think through pacing and homework load.

- Have students take notes during their discussions or fill out a text-agnostic graphic organizer, but do not create a text-specific assignment for them to complete. Their own insights and questions should drive each of their discussions.

Socratic Seminars

Consider having groups conduct a Socratic Seminar.

- Students create open-ended questions to ask each other during a formal discussion.

- The seminar should be student-led with little involvement from the teacher.

- Students' questions should build on each other's ideas and demonstrate their understanding of the text read.

- All students should participate. Evaluate their responses based on the insight and examples they provide.

How can I monitor students' independent reading?

Introduce Strategies and Let Students Do the Work

Providing students a chance to explore their own reading interests can engage them and encourage independence. Here are some suggestions for creating accountability.

- Meet with each student for a booktalk. Students should be prepared to talk about the main conflicts or ideas in the book, and give their opinions of them.

- Have students track and analyze **Notice & Note** signposts they identify while reading. They can use the **Notice & Note** Writing Frames to do so, or create a two-column chart with the signposts listed in one column and the examples and analysis in the other.

- Ask students to create dialectical journals. Have students identify significant quotations from the text in one column. In a second column, have students describe each quote's significance. Did it reveal something about the character or events? Did it impact the student's reading in some way?

Tips & Tricks!

Steer advanced learners toward higher Lexile® texts and challenge them to seek out and analyze competing critical perspectives.

Assessing Long Reads

How can I integrate skills/standards instruction with long reads?

Identify the Skills You Want to Reinforce

● If you're working with **Recommended Long Reads**, the **Study Guides** will include a list of skills that you can match with your standards. Otherwise, preview the text on your own.

● Consider teaching the core standards with the **Analyze & Apply** or **Collaborate & Compare** lessons in each unit. Then have students apply those skills and standards in their Literature Circles or in their independent reading of Long Reads.

● Reinforce the skills you want to teach with text-agnostic resources such as **Peer Coach**, **Skills Coach**, and graphic organizers that can be used across Literature Circles. Emphasize the skills you want the class to focus on by displaying anchor charts.

How can I assess what students have learned?

Choose and Customize

Use a combination of standardized assessment, writing-based assessment, and projects to understand what students have learned from their reading. *Into Literature* provides a variety of options depending on how closely you've woven the Long Reads into the unit themes and standards and whether you've used a **Recommended Long Read**.

● If you used the Long Read to connect to unit topic and themes, choose an end-of-unit task. The writing and speaking and listening opportunities allow students to demonstrate their understanding of how the book relates to the Essential Question. You can adapt the prompt to suit your needs.

● If you used the Long Reads to teach or reinforce the unit standards, customize the **Unit Tests** available on the platform. These are aligned to the reading, language, and vocabulary skills taught throughout the unit, and can be customized to eliminate any skills you haven't covered.

● If students read a Recommended Long Read, use the **Book Test** in the Study Guide, which is printable and available to assign on Ed. Use the Writing Prompts and Creative Projects available in the **Choices** section of the Study Guide. You can also assign the Extension activities on the **Reader's Choice** page of the Student Edition.

● If you've brought in an additional novel and taught it as a stand-alone unit, you may want to peruse the Writing Prompts and Creative Projects in the **Study Guides** to find assignments you can adapt to fit your purposes.

Tips & Tricks!

The **Media Projects** on Ed can often be adapted to work with a Long Read, providing an additional opportunity for students to demonstrate how the novel relates to the unit's Essential Question.

Student Engagement

54   Igniting Student Engagement

58   Integrating Social & Emotional Learning

Igniting Student Engagement

Knowing Your Audience

Remember—It's All About Them

Getting your students excited about reading literature starts with developing a deeper understanding of their interests.

> **How do I get my students to want to read literature?**

● At the beginning of the year, use an Interest Inventory to gain insights into students' favorite genres. Write a list of genres on a flip chart on the wall. Have students mark their three favorite genres in order of preference. Discuss their choices as a class. Another way to gauge students' preferences is to use polling software to create a survey. Use this information to select the texts you teach or recommend for independent reading.

● Before you start a new unit, use the **Spark Your Learning** feature—specifically, **Preview the Texts**—to see which titles generate the most interest and excitement. Review the titles, genres, and teasers as a class. Use a show of hands to see which title is most or least appealing. If you have flexibility in the texts you teach, or the order of those texts, use this insight to drive your planning.

What types of texts do you most like to read?

Love Stories	Adventure Stories
Historical Fiction	Mysteries
Graphic Novels/Comics	Science Fiction/Fantasy
Biography	Memoir
Poetry	Drama
Myths/Folklore	

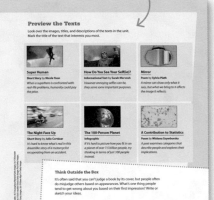

● Use the **Collaborate & Compare** feature in each unit to increase student engagement. Comparing classic and contemporary connections, different points of view, or various text formats can add interest and relevance to instruction.

Sparking Their Learning

Make the Connection

Into Literature was built with this question in mind. At the beginning of each unit and lesson, you will find a variety of options for hooking students and getting them invested in the learning. Try these suggestions:

● As a start to each unit, divide the class into small groups and prompt groups to discuss the opening illustration, along with the Analyze the Image question. Have each group share its ideas with the class.

● 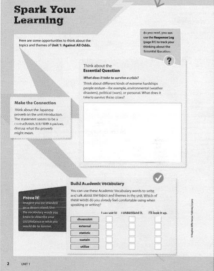 Play the **Stream to Start Video**, available in the **Student eBook**, to build students' knowledge about the unit topic.

● Use the activities in the **Spark Your Learning** feature at the beginning of the unit to brainstorm connections to pop culture and to get students thinking about the Essential Question. Consult the notes in your Teacher's Edition for flexible grouping ideas.

> **How do I ignite my students' interest in the topic or text that I'm about to teach?**

Tips & Tricks!

Use the annotation tools in your Teacher eBook to take notes and store any open-source links on current events or pop-culture connections.

● Browse for connections to current events on the **HMH Current Events** site, which is updated frequently.

● Launch each lesson in the unit with the **Engage Your Brain** activities, which are designed to get students sketching, quick-writing, and discussing key ideas related to the text.

> **How can I give my students choices, yet still accomplish my learning goals?**

Decide Which Kinds of Choice to Offer

Even if you are unable to let students' interests and choices dictate the texts you teach, you can still empower them with other kinds of choices. Here are some options:

- Have the class, small groups, or individuals select from the **Choices** activities at the end of each lesson.

- Invite students to choose how they will demonstrate their understanding of what they've learned in each unit. The writing and speaking and listening tasks are options, of course. Discover additional options in the **Reflect & Extend** feature at the end of each unit. One of those options is a **Media Project**, which is a great way to try out project-based learning in your classroom.

- Make sure to offer a variety of choices for independent reading connected to each unit. Start by consulting the **Reader's Choice** feature in the Student Edition for short and long reads that relate to the unit topic. Encourage students to preview the titles, genres, and teasers as they consider which options interest them.

- **Ed** Invite students to browse the **Text Library** on our learning platform for even more choices of novels, short stories, and informational texts on high-interest topics.

Going Beyond the Book Report

What are some high-interest ways for students to demonstrate what they learned in their independent reading?

Tips & Tricks!

Help students find their voice and confidence by having small groups frequently present their projects to the class. Require that each student in the group has a speaking part, even if it's only two sentences at the beginning.

Build in Creativity and Variety

Book reports are relics of the past. Today, there are countless creative ways—and digital tools—to help students share their independent reading with their class, their community, and the world. Such projects can tap into students' creativity and digital expertise, while increasing engagement along the way.

The **Reader's Choice** feature in each unit offers a variety of project ideas that you may want to explore. Here are a few ideas that can work equally well whether students are reading short texts, novels, or longer works of nonfiction.

Project Ideas:

Produce a Book Talk
A book talk is a short presentation about a book that persuades others to read it. Highlight aspects of the book that will intrigue potential readers.

Write a Text-Message Exchange
Create text messages between two characters, using knowledge of their motivations, ways of communicating, personalities, and relationships.

😊**Ed**

Spot Notice & Note Signposts
Find three Notice & Note signposts in a text. Use the **Writing Frames** online to go from identification to analysis and evaluation in writing.

Design a Social Media Profile
Create a social-media profile page for a character in a story. Include images, status updates, and comments that reflect that character's traits.

Create a Graphic Novel
Illustrate a key scene or event in a novel or short story.

Draft a Movie Script
Write a script that adapts a scene or event from a text. Consider how camera shots, sound effects, and music enhance the story.

Design a Book Jacket
Create a book jacket for a text, relying on layout, color, and text to communicate a mood or a theme. Include a summary or teaser that will make people want to buy the book!

Craft a Haiku
Write a haiku—an unrhymed poem of three lines of 5, 7, and 5 syllables each—that communicates something about a character, event, or theme of a text.

Draw a Sketchnote
A sketchnote is a form of visual note-taking that captures a text's main ideas in words and doodles. Create a sketchnote to remember key takeaways from any informational text or the plot of a fictional work.

Tweet It
Try the 280-character challenge! Craft a tweet that summarizes a key idea or theme of a text.

Create a Word Cloud
Record a cloud of words from a memoir or nonfiction narrative, with the title of the text in the center. Explain how the chosen words reflect the author's tone.

Produce a Podcast
Record a podcast discussion with two other classmates who read the same text. Share opinions of the text and the characters.

Integrating Social & Emotional Learning

Understanding the Competencies

What is social and emotional learning (SEL)?

Social & Emotional Learning

Social and Emotional Learning is the process by which people develop the ability to understand and manage emotions, set and achieve positive goals, feel and show empathy for others, establish and maintain positive relationships, and make responsible decisions.

Into Literature focuses on the core competencies of social and emotional learning developed by the Collaborative for Academic, Social, and Emotional Learning (CASEL).

SELF-AWARENESS

The ability to accurately recognize one's own emotions, thoughts, and values and how they influence behavior. The ability to accurately assess one's strengths and limitations, with a well-grounded sense of confidence, optimism, and a "growth mindset."

- Identifying Emotions
- Accurate Self- Perception
- Recognizing Strengths
- Self-Confidence
- Self-Efficacy

SELF-MANAGEMENT

The ability to successfully regulate one's emotions, thoughts, and behaviors in different situations—effectively managing stress, controlling impulses, and motivating oneself. The ability to set and work toward personal and academic goals.

- Impulse Control
- Stress Management
- Self-Discipline
- Self-Motivation
- Goal Setting
- Organizational Skills

SOCIAL AWARENESS

The ability to take the perspective of and empathize with others, including those from diverse backgrounds and cultures. The ability to understand social and ethical norms for behavior and to recognize family, school, and community resources and supports.

- Perspective-Taking
- Empathy
- Appreciating Diversity
- Respect for Others

RESPONSIBLE DECISION-MAKING

The ability to make constructive choices about personal behavior and social interactions based on ethical standards, safety concerns, and social norms. The realistic evaluation of consequences of various actions, and a consideration of the well-being of oneself and others.

- Identifying Problems
- Analyzing Situations
- Solving Problems
- Evaluating
- Reflecting
- Ethical Responsibility

RELATIONSHIP SKILLS

The ability to establish and maintain healthy and rewarding relationships with diverse individuals and groups. The ability to communicate clearly, listen well, cooperate with others, resist inappropriate social pressure, negotiate conflict constructively, and seek and offer help when needed.

- Communication
- Social Engagement
- Relationship Building
- Teamwork

HOMES & COMMUNITIES
SCHOOLS
CLASSROOMS

SELF-AWARENESS
SELF-MANAGEMENT
SOCIAL & EMOTIONAL LEARNING
SOCIAL AWARENESS
RESPONSIBLE DECISION-MAKING
RELATIONSHIP SKILLS

SEL CURRICULUM & INSTRUCTION
SCHOOLWIDE PRACTICES & POLICIES
FAMILY & COMMUNITY PARTNERSHIPS

Getting Started

It Helps Students Succeed

Why does SEL matter?

As an educator, you know that learning goes beyond acquiring facts and expanding knowledge. It's a personal journey that requires curiosity, perseverance, and growth. When students are taught the competencies and given opportunities to practice, they'll be better able to cope with the highs and lows of school and the learning process itself. Benefits include:

- Improved quality of teacher-student interactions
- Improved student performance
- Ease of social adjustments for students
- Increase in positive behaviors that result in positive outcomes
- Increase in supportive classroom culture

Start with Direct Instruction

Research shows that direct instruction in Social and Emotional Learning is effective. Make students aware of the concept early in the year.

How and when do I introduce my students to SEL?

- Start with a whole-class reading of **"The Most Important Subject Is You"** by Carol Jago, which appears on pages FM26–FM29 of the Student Edition.

- Consider using the content of the essay as a jumping-off point for a class discussion about how to foster a collaborative, supportive learning environment. Create anchor charts or other visual reminders of the key principles that emerge, such as having respectful conversations, valuing individual voices, managing emotions, and building relationships.

- Decide whether you want to introduce your students to the specific language of the competencies. These labels do not appear in the Student Edition, but the Teacher's Edition provides language to share with students at point of use as you see fit.

How can I connect SEL with my teaching of literature?

Use Unit Topics and Texts to Reinforce the Concepts

Research suggests that integrating SEL directly into the core curriculum is an effective practice. You can use the unit topics and selections to reinforce instruction of SEL concepts, and you can use SEL concepts to encourage students to analyze the selections through a different lens. *Into Literature* provides options for both, and plenty of opportunities for students to practice.

- In the **Introduce the Unit** feature, a Teacher's Edition note supports direct instruction in a specific competency.

- In the **Choices** section of every lesson, there's an activity in the Student Edition or the Teacher's Edition that connects the content of the literature to a competency.

Social & Emotional Learning
↳ Journal Entry

Think of an emotional or physical journey you have taken in your life. Maybe you had to move to a new school, went through a breakup, joined a team, or went on a trip. In a journal entry, describe the following:

- What obstacles did you have to overcome?

- How did others help or hinder your progress?

- What strengths did you discover in yourself? Did you learn things about yourself that you want to work on?

Social & Emotional Learning

Self-Awareness Our emotions, experiences, and unique point of view affect how we interpret and understand people and events in the world around us. Begin a class discussion by asking students to identify what they think they know about tenth grade and what they cannot know based on their point of view. Ask how their understanding and point of view may be different from a teacher's. Extend the discussion by having students work in small groups to make a poster that describes their understanding of tenth grade, emotions they feel about the school year, and how these emotions may affect their point of view. When finished, ask: How were you able to identify your emotions and point of view? What did you learn?

- In the **Reflect & Extend** section at the end of every unit, an SEL note in the Teacher's Edition provides guidance for incorporating an SEL competency into one of the activities.

- In the **Lesson Planning Guide**, every lesson that has an **SEL Choices** activity notes the SEL competency associated with it, so you can plan ahead. Selections that include especially sensitive content will have an additional note to provide you with suggestions and strategies for dealing with issues related to the text.

- The **Spark Your Learning** activities that open each unit and the **Engage Your Brain** activities that open each lesson provide opportunities for students to practice self-awareness, social awareness, and relationship skills.

- Text-based questions and writing activities encourage students to consider the factors and consequences involved in characters' decision-making, thus strengthening their own decision-making abilities.

Social & Emotional Learning

Reflect on the Essential Question Help students develop **social awareness** by responding to the questions and completing the sentence stems independently. Then have students work in small groups to interview each other about their responses.

- Circulate during these interviews to get a sense of students' thoughts.

- Wrap up with a whole-class discussion in which you reinforce key themes from the interviews.

- If you observe any consistent challenges that students encountered with the writing and presentation tasks, have students share strategies for overcoming them.

Providing Ongoing Support

> **What support is there for me as I navigate difficult topics and texts with my students?**

Preview and Communicate

Texts that allow students to develop empathy, contemplate life's challenges, and prepare for tough decisions can include sensitive material. It's not always possible to know what topics and content will provoke controversy or trigger trauma-based responses among individuals or groups. You know your students and communities best, so *Into Literature* provides you with ways to preview materials and adjust and prepare as you see fit. When students, parents, and guardians are informed about what the curriculum will include and why, they are more likely to respond positively.

- **⊙Ed** The **Build Family Engagement** note in the Teacher's Edition Unit Opener refers to an editable letter that can be sent to students' homes, providing an opportunity to preview and explain any potentially sensitive material that will be covered. You can find the letter on Ed, the learning platform.

- The **What Is This Story About?** note in each Teacher's Edition **Lesson Planning Guide** summarizes the selection so that you will be aware of the topics covered.

Social and Emotional Considerations

This story includes sensitive content. Use the Social & Emotional Learning activities in the Student and Teacher's Edition to help students explore ideas and issues related to this text.

⊙Ed Letter to Families About This Text

Sensitive Content	Context	SEL Approach
Physical abuse	Steve is routinely starved and beaten	The **Self-Management** activity on TE page 10 guides students to consider the skills that Steve employed.
Emotional abuse	Steve describes his foster family as very controlling.	The **Self-Awareness** activity on TE page 13 helps students think of sources of inspiration that help one feel hopeful.

Exploration and Reflection

Before reading, encourage students to think about the following questions to help them explore ideas related to the selection:

- **Social Awareness** How can physical abuse affect the way people interact with others? How can it change the way people feel about themselves?
- **Responsible Decision-Making** What should you do if you think that someone you know is experiencing abuse at home or bullying at school? What factors might make it hard to solve this type of problem?
- **Self-Awareness** What can people draw on for strength when they are in a painful or dangerous situation?

Then, after students have finished reading this selection, have them reflect on how their reading of the text has influenced their thinking.

What Is This Narrative About?

After serving as a child soldier in Sierra Leone, author Ishmael Beah was relocated to New York City and entered high school there. In his personal essay, Beah describes the challenges he faces to fit in with his classmates and the adjustments he makes to adapt to American teen culture. With great insight and understated wit, Beah describes his new life in and out of school, including a memorable weekend playing paintball. His experiences as a child soldier serve him well in paintball, but also keep him distant from his friends as he realizes he will never share their naïve innocence about the world.

⊙Ed Summaries in Other Languages

STUDENT ANTICIPATION GUIDE

Before Reading Before reading the book, mark your response to each item below in the "Before" column:

- Mark a plus sign (+) if you agree.
- Mark a minus sign (–) if you disagree.
- Mark a question mark (?) if you are unsure of your opinion.

Then freewrite about one of the items.

	BEFORE	AFTER
1. People should be punished when they do something wrong.		
2. Choices about how we live our own lives are our own business.		
3. Someone's first loyalty should be to his or her family.		
4. Things that seem risky should be avoided.		
5. If you get into trouble for helping someone, then they owe you.		

After Reading When you have finished reading and discussing the book, mark your responses to the items above in the "After" column. Then freewrite about one item. You may choose to write about

- the same item you chose for your Before Reading freewriting
- an item about which your opinion changed
- an item about which your opinion grew much stronger

- In the **HMH Study Guides,** a **Social and Emotional Considerations** section provides a chart showing potential triggering issues, and an **Anticipation Guide** prompts students to preview emotionally-charged elements of the text ahead of time to help prepare them.

> How can my school extend social and emotional learning beyond the *Into Literature* curriculum?

Try a Community Read with *A Chance in the World*

Social and emotional learning is especially effective when a whole school or whole grade commits to the process. HMH has partnered with author, speaker, and executive Steve Pemberton to create an SEL-focused curriculum around his inspirational memoir *A Chance in the World*. It's designed to engage students and bring communities together while fostering awareness of and growth in the CASEL core competencies.

The curriculum is appropriate for grades 8–12 and is built to be flexible. It can be used as

- an all-school read, with all students, teachers, and staff participating
- a summer read, which may include community library participation
- an all-grade read, perhaps for incoming or outgoing classes
- a core text in an ELA class, utilizing the optional academic component of the curriculum

READY TO TAKE A CHANCE?

Curriculum Guide
A Community Reading Experience

A CHANCE IN THE WORLD

We aren't measured by what happens to us but rather by how we respond to it.

–Steve Pemberton, author of *"A Chance in the World"*

USA TODAY Bestseller
Revised *and* Updated

NOW A MAJOR MOTION PICTURE

A CHANCE IN THE WORLD

An Orphan Boy, a Mysterious Past, and How He Found a Place Called Home

STEVE PEMBERTON

Providing Ongoing Support

Why this text?

It Engages Students and Explores Important Themes

A Chance in the World is a story of resilience, portraying Steve Pemberton's terrifying experiences in the foster-care system and his quest to uncover the truth about his origins. The memoir shines a harsh light on society's failure to protect vulnerable youths. Yet it also shows how acts of kindness can profoundly affect lives, and that we all have the potential to overcome adversity.

The book has moved and motivated many adolescents who see their own lives reflected in aspects of the author's experience. It encourages reflection on important questions: Where do I belong? How can I succeed when others dismiss my worth? How can I help those who need it?

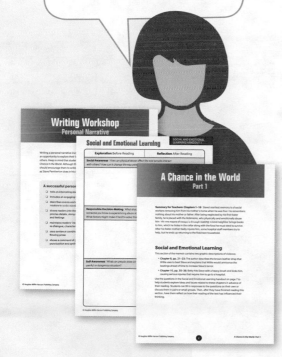

What does the curriculum include?

Social & Emotional Learning Resources and More

The **Curriculum Guide** was developed with input from educators who have successfully used *A Chance in the World* in their schools. The resources in it are also available digitally and supplemented by select digital-only assets. There are three sections.

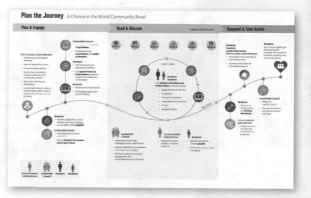

- **Plan & Engage** includes an experience map to help plan the journey, a letter to readers from Steve Pemberton, posters to generate excitement, and more.

- **Read & Discuss** divides the book into six parts. Each part contains a social and emotional learning activity, vocabulary, discussion questions, English language arts connections, suggested project ideas, and connections to related readings across multiple genres, which are included.

- **Respond & Take Action** includes culminating projects and an in-depth writing workshop on personal narrative.

Making *Into Literature* Work for You

Close Reading & Analysis

66   Using Notice & Note for Close Reading

72   Developing the Habits of Close Reading

Using Notice & Note for Close Reading

Getting Started

What is Notice & Note, and what are signposts?

Ⓝ NOTICE & NOTE

Notice & Note is a close-reading protocol grounded in the research of Dr. Kylene Beers and Dr. Robert E. Probst and designed to encourage students to be active readers. At the heart of Notice & Note are signposts—key aspects of literary and informational texts that are worth paying attention to. Each signpost is associated with an anchor question.

Kylene and Bob developed Notice & Note after studying the books most commonly taught in middle and high school. As they read, they noticed regularly-occurring features that helped them better understand key elements such as character development, internal conflict, and theme. They established three criteria that each feature had to meet in order to be taught to students:

1. It had to have a characteristic that made it noticeable, so that it could be identified.

2. It had to show up in a majority of works.

3. It had to help readers who noticed it understand something about their own responses or interpretations.

In response to student and teacher feedback, Kylene and Bob streamlined the signposts and anchor questions. Once they did, they noticed students adopting them more quickly, as well as generating more of their own questions—the ultimate goal. They later expanded into informational texts with similarly positive results.

Preview the Signposts

The chart you'll see when you turn the page includes the six literary signposts and five informational text signposts, plus the Big Questions that are important to ask when reading nonfiction.

How will Notice & Note help my students?

Draw Students Deep Into the Text

When students are taught to look for signposts and ask the anchor questions, they begin to read more thoughtfully. Through initial modeling and prompting, and then with increasing independence, students will make predictions and inferences based on text evidence and connect what they read with their own lives and the world around them.

Teachers report that signposts create rich fodder for conversation. Students of all levels can share the signposts they find in a text and debate their meaning, building on each other's ideas and sharing evidence that supports their interpretations. Instead of waiting for a teacher to guide them through the text, students begin to make their own meaning.

Learning by Example

The excerpts below are from the story "Thank You, M'am" by Langston Hughes. They contain several **Contrasts and Contradictions**, which are the most commonly-found signpost. The anchor question is "Why would the character act (or feel) this way?"

The annotations show a summarized version of how a teacher might work through a lesson after having introduced the signpost.

In the story, the boy has just tried to steal the woman's purse, and she's grabbed him.

"If I turn you loose, will you run?" asked the woman.

"Yes'm," said the boy.

"Then I won't turn you loose," said the woman. She did not release him.

"I'm very sorry, lady, I'm sorry," whispered the boy.

"Um-hum! And your face is dirty. I got a great mind to wash your face for you. Ain't you got nobody home to tell you to wash your face?"

"No'm," said the boy.

CC "Then it will get washed this evening," said the large woman starting up the street, dragging the frightened boy behind her.

MODEL

Here I pause and tell students the woman is acting in a way that contrasts with what I'd expect. If someone were trying to steal from me, I wouldn't invite them home to wash their face! So I'm going to ask why she would act that way. Is she feeling sorry for him? I'll have to keep reading to find out.

up the street. When she got to her door, she dragged the boy inside, down a hall, and into a large kitchenette-furnished room at the rear of the house. She switched on the light and left the door open. The boy could hear other roomers laughing and talking in the large house. Some of their doors were open, too, so he knew he and the woman were not alone. The woman still had him by the neck in the middle of her room.

She said, "What is your name?"

"Roger," answered the boy.

"Then, Roger, you go to that sink and wash your face," said the woman, whereupon she turned him loose—at last. Roger

CC looked at the door—looked at the woman—looked at the door—*and went to the sink.*

GUIDE

I tell students the contrast I noticed: Roger had been trying to get away, but now that he has the chance, he decides to stay. This time I ask students to pose the anchor question, and have them break into pairs for a minute or so to answer it. Students might offer a variety of reasons why he acts this way. I tell them that as we continue reading, they should mark a small CC next to any Contrasts and Contradictions they notice.

CC When they were finished eating she got up and said, "Now, here, take this ten dollars and buy yourself some blue suede shoes. And next time, do not make the mistake of **latching** onto *my* pocketbook *nor nobody else's*—because shoes come by devilish like that will burn your feet. I got to get my rest now. But I wish you would behave yourself, son, from here on in."

RELEASE

I invite students to share the most interesting CCs they noticed and share what they think about them. This usually leads to a rich conversation, as students dig into the characters' motivations and developments.

Close Reading & Analysis

CONTRASTS & CONTRADICTIONS

A sharp contrast between what we would expect and what we observe the character doing; behavior that contradicts previous behavior or well-established patterns

Why would the character act (feel) this way?

AHA MOMENT

A sudden realization of something that shifts a character's actions or understanding of self, others, or the world

How might this change things?

TOUGH QUESTIONS

Questions characters raise that reveal their inner struggles

What does this question make me wonder about?

WORDS OF THE WISER

The advice or insight about life that a wiser character, who is usually older, offers to the main character

What is the life lesson, and how might this affect the character?

AGAIN & AGAIN

Events, images, or particular words that recur over a portion of the story

Why might the author bring this up again and again?

MEMORY MOMENT

A recollection by a character that interrupts the forward progress of the story

Why might this memory moment be important?

Signposts for Informational Texts

BIG QUESTIONS

It's important to take a **Questioning Stance** or attitude when you read nonfiction.

- *What surprised me?*
- *What did the author think I already knew?*
- *What challenged, changed, or confirmed what I already knew?*

CONTRASTS & CONTRADICTIONS

A sharp contrast between what we would expect and what we observe happening; a difference between two or more elements in the texts

What is the difference and why does it matter?

EXTREME OR ABSOLUTE LANGUAGE

Language that leaves no doubt about a situation or an event, allows no compromise, or seems to exaggerate or overstate a case

Why did the author use this language?

QUOTED WORDS

Opinions or conclusions of someone who is an expert on the subject or someone who might be a participant in or a witness to an event; or the author might cite other people to provide support for a point

Why was this person quoted or cited, and what did this add?

NUMBERS AND STATS

Specific quantities or comparisons to depict the amount, size, or scale; or the writer is vague when we would expect more precision

Why did the author use these numbers or amounts?

WORD GAPS

Vocabulary that is unfamiliar to the reader—for example, a word with multiple meanings, a rare or technical word, or one with a far-removed antecedent

Do I know this word from someplace else? Can I find clues in the sentence to help me understand the word?

Introducing Students to Notice & Note

How do I introduce the signposts to my students?

Start with the Signposts

There's no one right way to introduce the signposts. Here are some tips to guide you.

● Start by having the whole class read and discuss the **essay** on pages FM22–FM25 of the Student Edition.

● Reserve time at the beginning of the school year to acquaint students with the signposts. Start by focusing on just one or two at a time.

● Consider the order. The signposts appear in the chart in order of the frequency with which they occur. Many teachers start with Contrasts and Contradictions, because selections often contain several of these. However, you may want to let the selection you're using drive the order. The **Lesson Overview** in the Teacher's Edition for each selection will tell you which signposts are covered.

● Consider using short film or television clips to introduce each signpost. On pages T28–T30, your Teacher's Edition suggests media examples that have worked for others.

● Connect with Kylene and Bob, as well as other devoted followers of Notice & Note, on social media. Find inspiring ideas and answers to common questions.

NOTICE & NOTE
Becoming a Better Reader

Reading is Change: Thoughts by Two Teachers
by Dr. Kylene Beers and Dr. Robert E. Probst

Dr. Kylene Beers

Dr. Robert E. Probst

In reading, as in almost everything else, paying attention is essential.

You wouldn't stand in the batter's box, facing a hard-throwing pitcher, with your mind wandering to what you may have for dinner that evening. The prospect of a fastball coming toward you at 80 miles an hour tends to focus the mind. And you wouldn't attempt to sing a difficult song in front of a large crowd with your thoughts on what you're going to wear to the dance this weekend. The need to remember the words, keep the beat, move to the rhythm, and stay in tune keeps you focused. When something counts, you pay attention. Close attention.

It's the same with reading. Of course, if you don't concentrate while reading, you won't suffer the pain of being knocked down by the fastball or the embarrassment of failing to hit the notes in front of the crowd. But if you don't pay attention as you read, there is barely any purpose in picking up the text at all.

But there is a purpose in reading, and that purpose is change.

We may read just to pass the time, to entertain ourselves when we have nothing to do. Or we might read simply to get information that we need. Where is tonight's game? What are the instructions for making the brownies? What's happening on whatever new app tells you what your friends are doing? The changes that result in these cases might be small (hopefully the brownies turned out better!), but they're still changes.

Other reading might enable us to change in much more significant ways.

You might . . .

● read about child labor in foreign countries and change your mind about what you will buy and what you will boycott.
● read The Hate U Give, and change your thinking about race and the justice system.
● read about climate change and wonder what you can do to help preserve the earth.

FM22 GRADE 9

How can I connect Notice & Note to skills and standards?

Connect to Curriculum

The "stickiness" of the signpost names can help students remember them. Yet, it helps to reinforce the direct connections between signposts and the academic language of literature. *Aha moment* is an epiphany; *again and again* is repetition.

Here are some ideas for making this connection:

● Point out the *Literary Analysis Connection* notes in the Student Edition Notice & Note handbook on pages R8–R13.

● Use the skills listed in the handbook to create a crosswalk between your standards and the signposts. This is a great way to reinforce Notice & Note within your ELA professional learning community.

Words of the Wiser

LITERARY ANALYSIS CONNECTION

Paying attention to Words of the Wiser can help you analyze

● theme
● internal conflict
● relationship between character and plot

After I teach a signpost, will students really be able to spot it on their own?

Tips & Tricks!

An expanded version of the chart appears on Student Edition pages FM24–FM25 and on Ed. Some teachers print and laminate the chart to use throughout the year during small-group work.

Reinforce and Practice with Signposts

Identifying signposts takes continued practice. Visual reminders help too. Here are some tips for keeping Notice & Note fresh in your students' minds.

- Display Notice & Note **Anchor Charts** describing each signpost on the wall.

- Print and distribute the bookmarks with descriptions of each signpost. Challenge students to use the Notice & Note annotation marks to identify signposts in their independent reading.

- Use the **Lesson Overview** in the Teacher's Edition to stay alert to opportunities to reinforce signposts within a lesson. As a bellringer activity, have students review the **Notice & Note Handbook** page for any signposts you'll be discussing in that day's lesson.

- Use the questions in the side margins of the Student Edition to model and guide close reading using signposts.

> **NOTICE & NOTE**
> **AGAIN AND AGAIN**
>
> When you notice certain words recurring over a portion of a text, you've found an **Again and Again** signpost.
>
> **Notice & Note:** Mark the word the Witches repeat in lines 48–69.
>
> **Analyze:** What is persuasive about their repetition?

45 Upon her skinny lips. You should be women,
And yet your beards forbid me to interpret
That you are so.

Macbeth. Speak, if you can. What are y[...]

First Witch. All hail, Macbeth! Hail to thee, Tha[...]

Second Witch. All hail, Macbeth! Hail to thee, [...]

50 **Third Witch.** All hail, Macbeth, that shalt be kin[...]

Banquo. Good sir, why do you start and seem t[...]
Things that do sound so fair? I' th' name of truth[...]

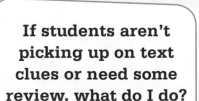

If students aren't picking up on text clues or need some review, what do I do?

Review the Signposts

It won't be long before your students are surprising you with all the signposts they discover in their reading. Every once in a while, though, it may help to review strategies for finding signposts. Here's how:

- Have students review the **Notice & Note Peer Coach videos** for the signposts they struggle with, or play them as a refresher for the whole class before a relevant lesson.

- Review with students the signposts and examples in the Student Edition **Notice & Note Handbook**.

Aha Moment
A sudden realization of something that shifts a character's actions or understanding of self, others, or the world

AHA! I GET IT NOW!

Extending & Enriching

How do I use Notice & Note with novels and long reads?

Scaffold and Release

Whether read by the whole class, as part of book groups, or independently, novels and memoirs are ideal texts in which to notice signposts, because they they include deep character development and long story arcs with multiple themes.

● If possible, model the discovery of a signpost in a novel before asking students to do so in groups or on their own. The chart on **Teacher's Edition** pages T28–T30 provides examples from Recommended Long Reads with which to model each signpost.

● Have students share the signposts they find with a small group or the class. Make sure they answer the anchor questions as part of their analysis.

● *Ed* Print and distribute the **Notice & Note Writing Frames** online. Prompt students to choose one signpost to focus on and analyze for other readers of the text. Challenge students to use the academic language of literature in their response.

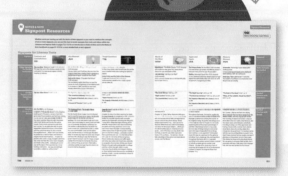

Is Notice & Note appropriate for advanced readers?

Apply to Complex Text

Notice & Note isn't something we grow out of as we become better readers. Rather, it can help us all analyze and appreciate the author's craft in the most daunting and complex texts. Signposts give students an accessible way to understand and analyze those texts, no matter how complex the syntax and ideas.

Developing the Habits of Close Reading

Getting Started

> **How can I promote more close reading in my classes?**

☺ **Ed**

Tips & Tricks!

If students don't have access to the printed book, they can mark up the eBook as they read. They can highlight and add notes directly to the text.

Built for Close Reading

Into Literature is built around close reading. The consumable format of the Student Edition invites students to be active readers, marking up the text as they go along. With ample margins and white space around each selection, students have the space they need to jot down notes and observations as they read—to look for things that you have asked them to find or simply to capture their own ideas, impressions, or questions.

At the beginning of the year, get students into the habit of recording informal notes as they read any text. For example, you might have them put:

- **?** a question mark next to ideas in the text they don't understand
- **✳** an asterisk next to surprising or important parts
- **!** an exclamation point to indicate ideas they disagree with
- **◯** a circle around unfamiliar words or phrases
- **LOL** an LOL! next to humorous characters, events, or ideas

Students should also get into the habit of doing more purposeful annotation, using the carefully crafted guided reading questions in the Student Edition. These questions prompt students to dig back into the text to look for specific skills-focused elements, fully aligned to the skills covered in the lesson.

Modeling Close Reading

> **How can I make sure that my students know what effective, purposeful annotation looks like?**

Show Annotation in Action

Into Literature doesn't just ask or invite students to annotate the text. The program also provides clear models of effective, purposeful annotation. Reviewing these models as a whole class can help students better understand what close reading looks and sounds like. Try these suggestions:

- At the start of every lesson, students will see an annotation model, **Annotation in Action**. It highlights one of the skills in the lesson and models effective text markup and annotation. Discuss this model before students read the text. As a next step, you might model the process as you read the first one or two paragraphs of the text aloud. Then invite volunteers to try it out on the next paragraphs.

The Tragedy of Macbeth
by William Shakespeare

Close Read Screencast 1

Annotation in Action

Here are one reader's notes about the Act I Prologue to *The Tragedy of Romeo and Juliet*. As you read, note clues about the play's setting, plot, and characters.

> Two households, both alike in dignity,
> In fair Verona, where we lay our scene,
> From ancient grudge break to new mutiny,
> Where civil blood makes civil hands unclean.
> From forth the fatal loins of these two foes,
> A pair of star-crossed lovers take their life,
> Whose misadventured piteous overthrows
> Doth with their death bury their parents' strife.

Foreshadowing — we already know how the play ends.

Close Read Practice Page

The Tragedy of Macbeth
by William Shakespeare

Do a close read of lines 9–18 in the selection by marking the text and answering the following questions.

The Tragedy of Macbeth	Close Read Notes
Lines 9–15	1. Underline descriptive **imagery**, or phrases appealing to the senses, in this section. What impressions do these descriptions create?
	2. Considering specific examples from the text, explain how—and why—Macbeth's relationship with *fear* has changed.
	3. What does Macbeth blame for this change? Consider the phrases *supped full with horrors* and *slaughterous thoughts*.

- **Ed** Certain texts in each unit feature **Close Read Screencasts**—modeled discussions about a key part of the text. You might view the screencast as a class and point out the kinds of details that the readers observe and discuss.

- **Ed** Students can hone their close-reading skills through frequent practice. Each text with a Close Read Screencast also includes a printable **Close Read Practice** activity, which is available on the platform. Have students complete the activity independently or in small groups.

- Extend the practice by having pairs of students record their own close read video about another part of text (their choice!) using screencast software.

How does *Into Literature* support close analysis and text-based responses?

UNIT 1

Response Log

Use this Response Log to record your ideas about how each of the texts in Unit 1 relates to or comments on the **Essential Question.**

ESSENTIAL QUESTION:
? **What does it take to survive a crisis?**

from A Chance in the World	
Is Survival Selfish?	

😊 *Ed*

Tips & Tricks!

If students use the digital annotation tools to mark evidence as they read, those annotations collect in the Notes panel of their eBook. Students can then review their annotations and Response Logs as they draft their writing for end-of-unit tasks. See **Building Better Writers** on page 78 to learn more about how the digital writing experience in **Writable** supports students in weaving evidence into their work.

Writable

Use the Text-Dependent Questions and Prompts

Close reading is just the start of reading and responding critically. In addition to getting your students to read the text closely and understand what an author is saying, you want them to analyze the texts and support their analysis and inferences with evidence from that text.

Into Literature provides a wealth of opportunities for students to demonstrate their close and careful reading. Here are some features you can use to build students' proficiency with text-dependent analysis.

- The **Analyze the Text** questions after each selection call on students to reach back into the text for evidence that supports their analysis. Whether you have students answer these questions in writing or as part of class discussion, challenge them to cite specific details to support their responses.

- Assign one or more of the **Choices** activities after reading. These activities focus on writing, media, speaking and listening, and research—and they require students to incorporate details from the text into their work.

- 😊 *Ed* Use the **Response Log**, located at the back of the Student Edition, to help students capture details from each text that relate to the Essential Question for the unit. Or students might use the interactive version on Ed. This practice sets students up for success on the end-of-unit writing task, which requires them to synthesize information and cite evidence from multiple texts.

Cite Evidence

3. In paragraph 4, the author states, "In the digital age, we're seeing more sophisticated limbs." What details does he provide in support of this main idea?

B I U F· ≡ ≡ 干· A· Ω

Start Typing...

Writing
↳ **Comparison**

Think about how the manga artist chose to portray the Witches, and evaluate the effect of this choice on the mood of the scene. Write a comparison, following these steps:

- Review Act I, Scene 3 of Shakespeare's play and make notes about how the characters of the Witches are portrayed. Note the historical and cultural context in which they appear.

- Make additional notes about how the manga version portrays the Witches and how the historical and cultural setting in which they appear differs. (If you watched the film clip in this unit, include that portrayal in your comparison as well.)

- Organize your ideas in a comparison-and-contrast structure to write a paragraph or two analyzing how the Witches are ... eir appearance and ... d cultural context add

Speaking & Listening
↳ **Small-Group Discussion**

"Harrison Bergeron" satirizes extreme and absurd methods used to achieve equality. Yet many groups and societies share the goal of equality under the law. Are they defining the term differently from the government's definition in the story?

Organize a group to discuss equality and how it can be achieved.

- Agree on a definition of equality the group will use.

- Cite examples of when individuals and groups have pushed governments toward greater equality.

- Acknowledge other perspectives or opinions in the group.

- Build on each other's ideas.

- Summarize your conclusions.

Close Reading and Notice & Note

> I'm interested in using Notice & Note as a close reading strategy. How does *Into Literature* support Notice & Note?

Complementary Approaches

Maybe you're already using Notice & Note as a close reading strategy. Or maybe it's something you've heard about and are interested to learn how to incorporate it into your close reading, without pulling you away from all the things you need to do, week to week. If so, *Into Literature* is the perfect program for you. Notice & Note is built right into our program.

Working closely with Notice & Note creators Kylene Beers and Robert Probst, *Into Literature* provides you with all the tools that you need to implement this accessible and powerful close reading protocol.

Use the resources in your Student and Teacher's Edition to get started with Notice & Note. Go online to find additional resources, from **Peer Coach Videos** and **Anchor Charts** to **Writing Frames for Fiction and Nonfiction**, to support and reinforce your instruction.

Tips & Tricks!

To learn more about using Notice & Note for close reading, see pages 66–71.

Aha Moment
A sudden realization of something that shifts a character's actions or understanding of self, others, or the world

AHA! I GET IT NOW!

N NOTICE & NOTE
AHA MOMENT

When you notice a sudden realization, you've found an **Aha Moment** signpost.

Notice & Note: Mark what Banquo and Macbeth realize in lines 107–120.

Predict: How might this change things?

105 He bade me, from him, call thee Thane of Cawdor,
In which addition, hail, most worthy thane,
For it is thine.

Banquo. What, can the devil speak true?

Macbeth. The Thane of Cawdor lives. Why do you dress me
In borrowed robes?

Angus. Who was the Thane lives yet,
110 But under heavy judgment bears that life
Which he deserves to lose. Whether he was combined
With those of Norway, or did line the rebel
...t with both
...now not;

N NOTICE & NOTE
Signposts

When you notice a signpost in your reading, mark the text with its initials.

LITERARY TEXTS

CONTRASTS AND CONTRADICTIONS CC
A sharp contrast between what we would expect and what we observe the character doing; behavior that contradicts previous behavior or well-established patterns

When you notice this signpost, ask:
Why would the character act/feel this way?
p. R8

AHA MOMENT AM
A sudden realization of something that shifts a character's actions or understanding of self, others, or the world

When you notice this signpost, ask:
How might this change things?
p. R9

TOUGH QUESTIONS TQ
Questions characters raise that reveal their inner struggles

When you notice this signpost, ask:
What does this question make me wonder about?
p. R10

WORDS OF THE WISER WW
The advice or insight about life that a wiser character, who is usually older, offers to the main character

When you notice this signpost, ask:
What is the life lesson, and how might this affect the character?
p. R11

AGAIN AND AGAIN AA
Events, images, or particular words that recur over a portion of the story

When you notice this signpost, ask:
Why might the author bring this up again and again?
p. R12

MEMORY MOMENT MM
A recollection by a character that interrupts the forward progress of the story

When you notice this signpost, ask:
Why might this memory moment be important?
p. R13

INFORMATIONAL TEXTS

BIG QUESTIONS BQ
It's important to take a **Questioning Stance** or attitude when you read nonfiction.

- *What surprised me?*
- *What did the author think I already knew?*
- *What challenged, changed, or confirmed what I already knew?*
p. R14

CONTRASTS AND CONTRADICTIONS
A sharp contrast between what we would expect and what we observe happening; a difference between two or more things in the text

When you notice this signpost, ask:
What is the difference, and does it matter?

NUMBERS AND STATS NS
Specific quantities or comparisons to depict the amount, size, or scale; or the writer is vague and imprecise about numbers when we would expect more precision

When you notice this signpost, ask:
Why did the author use these numbers or amounts?

QUOTED WORDS
Opinions or conclusions of someone who is an expert on the subject or someone who was a participant in or an eyewitness to an event; or the author quotes other people to provide support for a point

When you notice this signpost, ask:
Why was this person quoted or cited, and what did the author...
p. R17

FM24 GRADE 9

Ed
Peer Coach Videos

Notice ⓝ Note WHAT'S HAPPENING

Contrasts and Contradictions

When you're reading and the author shows you a difference between what you know and what is happening in the text or a difference between two or more things in the text, you should stop and ask yourself:

"What is the difference and why does it matter?"

The answer will help you see details that show you the main idea, compare and contrast, understand the author's purpose, infer, make a generalization, notice cause and effect.

Outcomes & Growth

78   Building Better Writers

84   Integrating Speaking & Listening

88   Integrating Grammar and Vocabulary
        into Your Lessons

94   Assessing Student Progress & Mastery

Getting Started

I'm not experienced at teaching writing. Help!

Into Literature Has You Covered

If you lack confidence in your ability to teach writing, you're not alone. It's a challenge for most of us to put well-crafted sentences and paragraphs on paper, let alone teach others how to do it well. Yet, with the right resources and tools, you can succeed. (Yes, *really*.)

Those writing resources and tools are built into every aspect of *Into Literature*. Here are some ideas for using the resources in the program to build writing into your daily classroom routines.

- **Kick off with quickwrites.** Begin each unit by having students quickwrite in response to the illustration and the Essential Question. Students can jot down their ideas within the **Spark Your Learning** pages in the Student Edition. Quickwriting is also an effective way to launch each lesson. Find inspiration and prompts within the **Engage Your Brain** feature at the start of each lesson.

- **Offer opportunities to write about the reading.** The **Respond** section after each lesson in the Student Edition includes a variety of writing activities. Students can write in response to the **Analyze the Text** questions or the **Choices** prompts that follow.

- **Build toward a cumulative task.** The writing task at the end of each unit prompts students to synthesize what they've learned across the texts and share new insights in different modes, including arguments, expository texts, and narratives. Students can prepare for this end-of-unit task by recording notes about the Essential Question in their **Response Logs**, located in the back of the Student Edition.

- 😊 **Ed** **Use Writable.** All of the writing assignments within the Student Edition—plus a library of additional connected prompts—are available in **Writable**, which you can access from Ed: Your Friend in Learning. Writable's peer review function drives the revision process, which helps students grow as writers. And time-saving tools like Revision Aid and Turn It In support teachers.

Connecting Reading & Writing

Share Models and Examples

One effective way to connect reading and writing is to expose students to strong models of each form. The instructional design of *Into Literature* helps you make that connection.

> **What tips do you have for closely connecting reading and writing?**

- Each unit includes one or more **mentor texts**—authentic examples of the form that students are responsible for writing as part of the cumulative task. As students read and analyze the mentor texts, they are prompted to look at aspects of the writer's craft.

- The end-of-unit task reinforces this reading-writing connection by having students revisit specific techniques used by the writers of the mentor texts. Challenge students to use these techniques in their own writing.

- **Ed** The **Interactive Writing Lessons** on our platform include examples—both strong and weak—of student writing. Consider projecting these models and using them in a whole-class discussion and peer review.

Review the Prompt and Rubric

Take the time to familiarize students with the destination before they embark on each end-of-unit writing journey. Here's how:

> **How can I make sure my students know what's expected of their writing?**

- As a class, review the writing prompt at the beginning of the task. Ask: What is the purpose and format of the writing? Who is the audience? Encourage students to underline or circle key details in the prompt that clarify the assignment.

- Examine each bulleted characteristic in the rubric on second page of the task. Explain any unfamiliar terms to students, and invite them to offer examples.

- Review the mentor text, depending on how recently you taught it. Consider asking students to explain how the mentor text exemplifies different characteristics listed in the rubric.

Tips & Tricks!

Writable

Assign the **Analyze the Mentor Text** prompt in each unit to inspire deeper analysis of writer's craft.

> **How can I help students write argumentative and expository texts?**

Provide Frequent Practice

Writing effective arguments and expository texts is critically important—for success on high-stakes assessments, in college, and in the workplace. You can help students achieve success by giving them frequent practice in these modes.

- If you preview all the prompts and tasks within *Into Literature*, you'll notice more opportunities to write arguments and expository texts than other forms. Look for occasions to change the focus or complexity of instruction at different points in the year. For instance, if students are writing an argument in September, they might focus on the basics—claim, support, and counterclaims. An assignment later in the year might challenge students to use rhetorical devices for persuasive effect.

- Use the scaffolding and graphic organizers in the Student Edition to support students in honing their skills in these modes.

- **⊙Ed** Prepare students for the cumulative task by assigning only prompts in that form over the course of the unit. Within **Writable**, you will find an additional prompt for each text that "ladders up" to the end-of-unit task.

Exploring Your Options

> **What if I don't like the end-of-unit task for a specific unit?**

Consider the Alternatives

Don't feel limited by the writing task or mode featured in each unit. *Into Literature* has alternatives for those who want to chart a different course.

- Consult the end-of-unit task **Planning Guides** in your Teacher's Edition for a list of other cumulative assignments you might consider.

- Check the **Reflect & Extend** feature in the Student Edition for a writing prompt focused on a different mode. If you are looking for more instruction to support the assignment, use the **Interactive Writing Lessons** on the platform.

- The **Reflect & Extend** feature also includes a unit **Media Project**—a great opportunity to experiment with project-based learning in your classroom. Find step-by-step support for each project online. Even if you lack the technology or the time to devote to an extended project, you might assign a low-tech or no-tech option. Storyboarding, scripting, and sketchnoting are all valuable writing opportunities for students.

- **⊙Ed** Can't find what you are looking for? Create your own prompt or assignment in **Writable**.

Alternate Tasks

See page 298B for resources for using these prompts to assess students' understanding of the unit.

- Write a Short Story
- Create an Infographic

Supporting Students with Key Skills

How do I help my students with tricky skills like citing text evidence and synthesizing across texts?

HMH
PEER COACH
Alex
CITE TEXT EVIDENCE

Reinforce the Fundamentals

Even seasoned writers can struggle with skills like citing text evidence and synthesizing across texts. Carve out class time to provide targeted teaching and practice in these fundamental skills. Here are some resources in the program that can help you:

Citing Text Evidence

- As a class, review the **Peer Coach Video** on citing text evidence. Then have students practice the **ACE** method—**A**nswer, **C**ite, **E**xplain. Encourage them to use this method when jotting down brief responses to questions about the texts they are reading, as well as in more formal writing assignments.

- Display the **Anchor Chart** that accompanies the Peer Coach video as a visual reminder of this method. Find a printable version of the chart on Ed. Consider also displaying some sentence starters that students can use to weave text evidence into their writing. As a class, brainstorm additional sentence starters to add to the sticky notes shown.

In the first paragraph, the text states that . . .

The writer emphasizes that . . .

According to the text, . . .

These lines prove that . . .

By stating . . . . the writer asserts . . .

- For independent practice, assign **Interactive Writing Lessons: Using Textual Evidence**.

Synthesizing Across Texts

- To review the skill, show the **Peer Coach Video** on synthesis, as well as printing and distributing the corresponding **Anchor Chart**.

- At the beginning of each unit, review the **Response Log** in the back of the Student Edition. Then, after students read each text, have them revisit the Essential Question, using the chart to note how that text relates to the question. Prompt them to record their opinions and insights, as well as direct quotations from the text. This practice will set students up for success in synthesizing information across the texts as part of the cumulative writing task.

- Use the **Collaborate & Compare** lessons in each unit to help students practice synthesizing information across two texts. The project at the end of the **Collaborate & Compare** gives students the perfect opportunity.

Tips & Tricks!

Have students record notes in the interactive **Response Log** in their eBooks. They can also use the annotation tools to capture additional notes as they read each text. **Writable** allows students to view those notes alongside their draft to support them in synthesizing information and citing text evidence.

Synthesize Information

RECIPE FOR SYNTHESIS
- Take two or more sources.
- Look at what they have in common. Where do the ideas overlap?
- Blend the most relevant information together.
- Mix in your own thoughts and ideas.

INFO IDEAS INFO IDEAS INFO

REMEMBER, synthesizing is more than comparing. You need to add your own ideas to say something new.

What are the best ways for students to get feedback on their work?

Build in Time for Self, Peer, and Teacher Review

Rarely (or ever!) does a first draft reflect the well-reasoned argument or suspenseful narrative we envisioned so clearly in our minds. Writing is a process: Our words, sentences, and ideas gain power and precision through extensive revision. That revision can be inspired by our own "fresh read" of our draft and by helpful suggestions from peers.

Here are some steps you can take to establish a culture of feedback in your classroom.

Self Review

- Build in class time for students to review their own drafts. The **Revision Guide** for each end-of-unit writing task in the Student Edition breaks down this process. Use the **Peer Review in Action** feature to model how to use the Revision Guide.

- **Ed** If students are using **Writable** to complete their drafts, remind them to consult the writer's checklist before they submit their work.

- For major writing assignments, use one or two class periods for a "revise-a-palooza" activity. Set up stations around the classroom, with each station focused on a different aspect of writing—introduction, body paragraphs, conclusion, elaboration, transitions, and so on. Have small groups of students spend 10 minutes at each station, revising their drafts with that focus.

Peer Review

- As a class, generate a list of sentence starters that students can use when they review their peers' drafts. Display these sentence starters on the wall. Ask students to use several of the starters each time they undertake a peer review.

I really liked how you...

I was a little confused when you said... because....

One way to grab your readers' attention would be to...

Another piece of evidence you can include is...

Your writing would be easier to understand if you added transitions like...

Your organization would be clearer if you...

- **Ed** Use the anonymous peer-review function in **Writable** to add an element of fun to the process of revision. Set up the assignment so that each student reviews the drafts of multiple peers. Encourage reviewers to use the comment stems to provide concrete feedback. Then challenge students to use their classmates' suggestions to revise their work.

Conferences

- Make the time to confer with your students about their drafts. Use the **Quick Check** prompts in your Teacher's Edition to support your students at each stage of the end-of-unit writing task.

- You might circulate around the room as you check in on individuals. Another option is to meet with each student as the rest of the class participates in peer review or "revise-a-palooza."

😊 **Ed**

Saving Time

How can I spend less time grading student writing?

Set Yourself Up for Success

Ever feel buried under the weight of student essays waiting for your review? If you let yourself, you can spend your weekends and evenings trying to keep up with the onerous job of grading student writing. Don't do it! Instead, use these practical tips, tools, and tricks to make grading more manageable.

- **Don't grade every assignment.** Reserve grading for major assignments, such as end-of-unit writing tasks and practice for summative assessments. For lower-stakes assignments, such as **Choices** prompts after each lesson, peer and self review can suffice.

- **Rely on peer review.** Remember—peer review can also help *you*. The comments, feedback, and ratings of peers can serve as a gauge for you to consider in your grading of major assignments.

Writable

- **Leverage time-saving digital tools.** The tools embedded within **Writable** are designed to make grading a little bit easier for you. Activate **Turn It In** to check the originality of students' work. Consult AI-powered **Revision Aid** to get paragraph-level feedback on the ideas, organization, and language in each draft. Use the comment stems provided to help you compose your feedback. You can also create your own comment stems for future use.

- **Use data and reports.** Let the data drive the focus of your review. Use the reports in **Writable** to track students' proficiency with skills connected to standards. Then use this targeted lens to grade students' writing assignments.

Integrating Speaking & Listening

Getting Started

How can I make sure that my students have productive discussions about literature?

Engage Their Brains

As a comprehensive literature program, *Into Literature* contains ample instructional support and abundant opportunities for speaking and listening. We know that in a typical week, a sizable part of your classroom time is spent having discussions. By using *Into Literature's* features, you can ensure that students have productive discussions that are not only helping them master ELA concepts but also building their competency in communicating ideas clearly and responding to ideas that might be very different from their own.

- At the beginning of the year, do a whole-class reading of the essay **"The Most Important Subject Is You"** by Carol Jago, which appears in the Student Edition on pages FM26–FM29. Review and discuss the strategies for effective conversations and discussions. Generate ground rules for your classroom community, which you may want to display on the wall.

- Use the **Spark Your Learning** and **Engage Your Brain** activities at the beginning of each unit and lesson to hook and engage students. These brief, informal opportunities for discussion can help to ease students into the lesson or make personal connections to ideas in the text.

Social & Emotional Learning

The Most Important Subject Is You!
by Carol Jago

You have essays to turn in. You have quizzes to take. You have group projects to complete. Your success in those areas depends on more than your understanding of the academic skills they cover. It also depends on how well you understand yourself, and how well you're able to extend that understanding to others. This might seem obvious, but there's an actual term for that type of learning—it's called **Social and Emotional Learning.**

Why It Matters

But doing well in school is not the only benefit to understanding yourself and others. When it comes to Social and Emotional Learning, the answer to the question, "When will I actually use this in my life?" is clear: every single day, forever. Whether you are with your family, your community, your friends, at a workplace, or by yourself on a deserted island, you will have a better chance of achieving satisfaction and making positive contributions if you're able to do things like the following:

- ✓ identify your emotions
- ✓ make smart choices
- ✓ set reasonable goals
- ✓ recognize your strengths
- ✓ have empathy
- ✓ manage your reactions
- ✓ evaluate problems and solutions
- ✓ show respect for others

FM28 GRADE 8

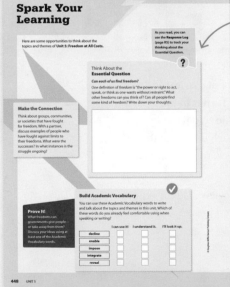

Spark Your Learning

Here are some opportunities to think about the topics and themes of **Unit 5: Freedom at All Costs.**

As you read, you can use the **Response Log** (page 85) to track your thinking about the **Essential Question.**

Think About the Essential Question

Can each of us find freedom?

One definition of freedom is "the power or right to act, speak, or think as one wants without restraint." What other freedoms can you think of? Can all people find some kind of freedom? Write down your thoughts.

Make the Connection

Think about groups, communities, or societies that have fought for freedom. With a partner, discuss examples of people who have fought against limits to their freedoms. What were the successes? In what instances is the struggle ongoing?

Prove It!

What freedoms can governments give people—or take away from them? Discuss your ideas using at least one of the Academic Vocabulary words.

Build Academic Vocabulary

You can use these Academic Vocabulary words to write and talk about the topics and themes in this unit. Which of these words do you already feel comfortable using when speaking or writing?

	I can use it!	I understand it.	I'll look it up.
decline			
enable			
impose			
integrate			
reveal			

448 UNIT 5

Engage Your Brain

Choose one or more of these activities to start connecting with the poem you are about to read.

Historical Backdrop

Wisława Szymborska was born in Poland in 1923. Research the experience of the Polish people during World War II. Then talk with a partner about how a young poet might have been affected by Poland's role in the war.

War Zones

With a partner, do some quick research on areas of the world with ongoing wars or conflicts.
1. Identify at least three regions or countries currently at war.
2. Explain the causes behind the conflicts.
3. Compare your findings with another pair.

- After students finish reading each text, have them discuss the **Collaborative Discussion** prompt with a classmate. Encourage sharing of ideas and perspectives in a whole-class discussion before moving on to more sophisticated textual analysis.

Talking About the Text

How can I use speaking and listening to support more in-depth analysis of a text?

Make Time for More Structured Activities

Informal classroom discussions can be a great way to get the ball rolling, but students can also use more formal, structured opportunities to practice higher-level skills. After every selection, in the **Choices** section, you will always have an option to assign a speaking and listening activity as an end-of-selection assessment. These activities are more stepped-out and structured, containing suggestions for purposeful speaking and effective and constructive listening.

Notice that many of these activities also support social and emotional learning. Speaking and listening activities are great opportunities for students to work on SEL competencies.

Speaking & Listening
↳ **Propose a Solution**

Gather information about the U.S. asylum process, including testimonials from asylum seekers. What about the process works well? How do you think it could be improved? Propose a solution to one problem with the process that you identify, considering all of the agencies and people
ies of the

Social & Emotional Learning
↳ **Group Discussion**

With a small group, discuss how the memoir "The Hawk Can Soar" relates to the theme of Hard-Won Liberty. In what way is the author striving for freedom? In your discussion, each group member should

- take turns and listen respectfully, asking questions for clarification as needed
- share evidence from the text to justify your views
- identify a personal connection with the author's situation
- respond to and build on each other's ideas, adjusting your own view if warranted

Ed

Share Models and Examples

Speaking and listening are skills that you have to see in action to fully understand. That makes *Into Literature's* speaking and listening interactive lessons a vital part of our coverage. Encourage students to go online to see instruction and models of effective collaboration, discussion, and presenting. Or, you might share these models in a whole-class lesson. Have students identify characteristics of strong discussions and presentations.

What Does a Collaborative Discussion Sound Like?

Listen in on this small group discussion, a meeting of the members of a class discussion group. See if you can spot students' constructive—and disruptive—discussion behaviors.

| ▶ 00:00/01:28 ● ──────────── ◁》 |
| 1. Show Up Ready   01:28 |

What Makes a Dynamic Presentation?

This speaker was assigned to give an informal demonstration of the verbal and nonverbal elements of speech delivery. View each segment of her presentation and respond to the questions.

> **How can I promote more collaboration in my classroom?**

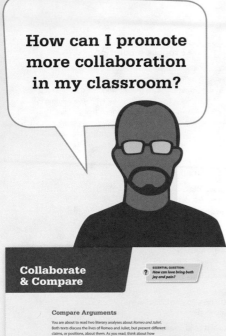

Collaboration: A Skill for the Future

Whether you're teaching middle school or high school, you know that you have to prepare students for a future in which collaboration is going to be a key to success. The ability to work effectively in teams is growing in importance, both in college and on the job. Your ELA classroom is where students will receive some of the best and more relevant practice with this skill.

An entire strand of *Into Literature*—**Collaborate & Compare**—supports collaborative group work. Students are still asked to read and analyze each text on their own or with the entire class. But as a final wrap-up assignment, they will work together as a team on a collaborative project. All of these projects require that students hone their speaking and listening skills.

Keep the following tips in mind when using these collaborative activities in your classroom.

- **Make the time.** These lessons take precious instructional time, but they are worth it. Students have the opportunity to flex various muscles, from collaboration and synthesis to research and presentation.

- **Keep peer groups small.** Each group should contain between four and six students. Smaller sizes allow for more focused collaboration, with each student playing a critical role in the work.

- **Let groups showcase their work.** Build in time for presentation, sharing, and reflection at the end of the assignment. Groups should feel proud of their work!

Using Speaking and Listening in Summative Tasks

> **How can I get students to engage in more extended speaking and listening activities?**

Tips & Tricks!

Each end-of-unit speaking and listening task includes point-of-use links to more support and instruction. Students can use these digital resources to find extra help, or you might use the resources to deliver a whole-class minilesson on relevant speaking and listening skills.

It Doesn't Have to Be a Writing Assignment

A lot of students don't like to write papers—probably most of them, in fact. But you know that some students in your class love to get up and talk in front of the class or engage in a spirited debate. And some students need more practice in these areas. With *Into Literature*, the end-of-unit assignment doesn't have to be another paper. It can be something that allows some of your more outspoken students to shine, and that gives some of your quieter students a clear and structured assignment to nudge them out of their comfort zone and to help them on their way to becoming poised and confident presenters.

Speaking & Listening

Participate in a Collaborative Discussion

Throughout this unit you have analyzed what drives—or inspires—people to take on a challenge. Now you will synthesize your ideas by participating in a collaborative discussion on the topic of how different people meet the need for challenges in life.

Use Your Essay as the Basis for Participation

Review your essay, and use the chart below to guide you as you make notes for the collaborative discussion.

	Notes for Collabo...
Key Point	
Key Point	
Key Point	

Speaking & Listening

Deliver a Multimedia Presentation

Consider your answer to the Essential Question: *How does our point of view shape our view of the world?* Create and present a 3- to 5-minute multimedia presentation that reflects on different points of view on an issue or problem.

Plan Your Presentation

Your presentation should focus on a clear thesis statement and strong key ideas. Think of strategies that will help you engage and inform your audience.

Use the chart to guide you as you plan your presentation. Then refer to the chart as you draft a script and combine your audio, visual, and graphic elements using presentation software.

Engage Your Audience
- Select ideas for which

	Presentation Plannin...
What is the thesis of my presentation?	
What key ideas will best support my thesis?	
What visuals and graphics will add interest and support my key ideas?	
What music or sound effects will help convey my ideas?	

Speaking & Listening

Produce a Podcast

You have written a compelling story that illustrates a conflict involving nature. Now you will share your ideas with a whole new audience by adapting it into a podcast. You will also listen to the podcasts created by your classmates, ask questions to better understand their goals, and help them improve their audio stories.

Plan Your Podcast

Review your story and complete the chart to help you adapt it for a podcast. Your podcast will spice up your story text by adding elements such as music and sound. You might also make your story more engaging for listeners by eliminating descriptive passages or slow parts. Use your answers to write the script you will follow to produce your podcast.

Questions	Answers and Notes
How will you capture listeners' attention right from the beginning?	
Will you tell the whole story, or will you have classmates read the dialogue in character?	
What audio elements can create the mood you want? Where will background music or sound effects add interest or emotion?	
How will you pace your reading to build tension or humor? Which parts will you read faster or slower?	

Produce a Podcast **587**

Integrating Grammar and Vocabulary into Your Lessons

Getting Started

How does *Into Literature* help me teach grammar and vocabulary in context?

Tips & Tricks!

If you are new to the classroom, integrating grammar and vocabulary into the study of literature may seem daunting. Don't despair! The hard work is finding meaningful integration points with literature, and we've done that for you. If you rely on the support in the Student and Teacher's Edition, you've got everything you need.

An Integrated Approach

Grammar and vocabulary are integrated directly into our program. Coverage begins with the Student Edition. Every prose selection in the Student Edition contains a complete grammar lesson on a topic or concept drawn from an authentic text. Also, carefully chosen "words to learn" help students expand their vocabulary as they read.

This integrated approach to grammar and vocabulary sets you up for instructional success. With instruction and practice specifically integrated into each lesson, students have meaningful opportunities to relate grammar and word choice to author's craft.

Watch Your Language!

Use Appositives Effectively

An **appositive** is a noun or pronoun that identifies or renames another noun or pronoun. An **appositive phrase** includes an appositive and its modifiers.

An appositive can be either essential or nonessential. An essential appositive provides information that is needed to identify what is referred to by the preceding noun or pronoun.

Watch Your Language!

Noun Clauses

A **clause** is a group of words that contains a subject and a verb. A clause may be **independent**, meaning it can stand alone as a sentence, or **dependent**, meaning it cannot stand alone. Dependent clauses act as modifiers that add meaning to independent clauses and often begin with subordinating conjunctions such as *since, that, though, until, where, while, who,* and *why*.

A noun clause is a type of dependent clause that functions as a noun in a sentence. Noun clauses may be introduced by words such as *why, whoever, what,* and *how*. Note the way each noun clause functions in these examples:

Expand Your Vocabulary

Put a check mark next to the vocabulary words that you feel comfortable using when speaking or writing.

irrefutable	☐
insidious	☐
atrophy	☐
contemptuous	☐
occult	☐

Turn to a partner and talk about the vocabulary words you already know. Then, write a social media post about a time when you faced an obstacle of some sort, using as many of the vocabulary words as you can. As you read "The Hawk Can Soar," use the definitions in the side column to help you learn the vocabulary words you don't already know.

Expand Your Vocabulary

PRACTICE AND APPLY

Answer the questions to show your understanding of the vocabulary words.

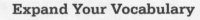

| irrefutable | insidious | atrophy | contemptuous | occult |

1. What is an **irrefutable** fact about life?

2. What is a problem that you would consider **insidious**?

3. What is a reason why a muscle might **atrophy**?

4. Why might someone act **contemptuous**?

5. What is **occult** about computer programming?

Ed

Diving More Deeply Into Grammar

What if I want to dig deeper into a grammatical topic?

A Systematic Approach

Sometimes, it helps to reinforce grammatical concepts outside the context of literature. After all, that's where students can get deeper instruction and practice. *Into Literature* contains a full online grammar, usage, and mechanics program—**Interactive Grammar Lessons**—covering the full range of topics. Each lesson contains clear, direct instruction (with models and examples) and a full range of engaging practice opportunities that provide immediate and clear feedback to students.

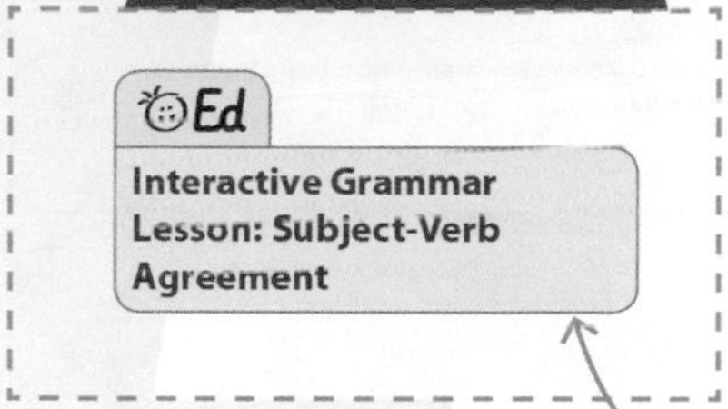
Ed
Interactive Grammar Lesson: Subject-Verb Agreement

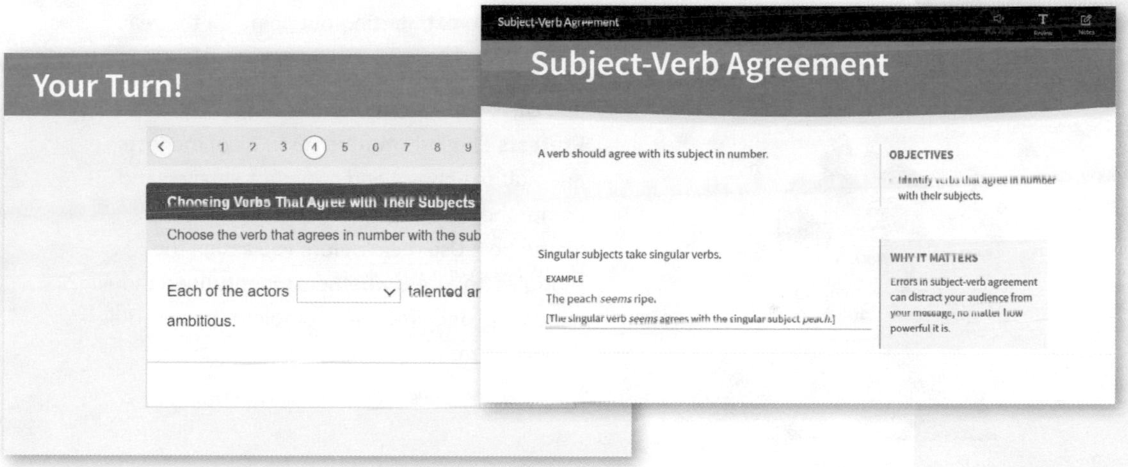
Your Turn!
1 2 3 4 5 6 7 8 9
Choosing Verbs That Agree with Their Subjects
Choose the verb that agrees in number with the sub
Each of the actors talented ar
ambitious.
Subject-Verb Agreement
Subject-Verb Agreement
A verb should agree with its subject in number.
OBJECTIVES
Identify verbs that agree in number with their subjects.
Singular subjects take singular verbs.
EXAMPLE
The peach seems ripe.
[The singular verb seems agrees with the singular subject peach.]
WHY IT MATTERS
Errors in subject-verb agreement can distract your audience from your message, no matter how powerful it is.

Throughout the Student Edition, there are point-of-use references to these online tutorials, which allow students to get valuable reteaching opportunities or extra practice.

Into Literature also offers the **Grammar Practice Workbook**. This student consumable contains all of the topics covered in the online grammar program, but in a friendly format, so that students can practice wherever and whenever they want. Each lesson begins with a quick refresher on the topic, followed by grade-appropriate practice. The lessons are also available as editable Word files, so that you can customize and adapt them as you see fit.

HMH
into Literature
Grammar Practice
Grade 9

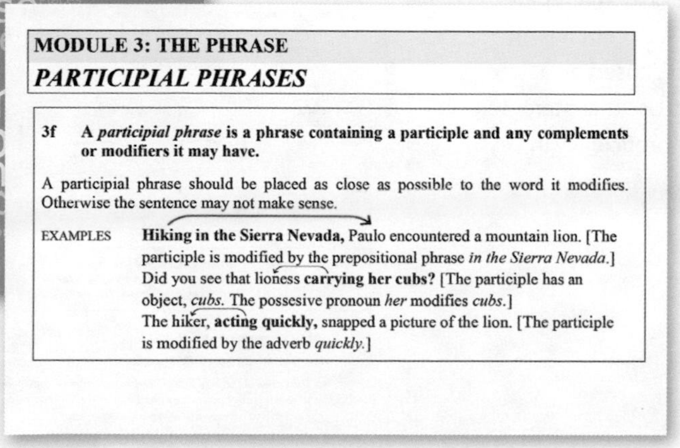

MODULE 3: THE PHRASE

PARTICIPIAL PHRASES

3f **A *participial phrase* is a phrase containing a participle and any complements or modifiers it may have.**

A participial phrase should be placed as close as possible to the word it modifies. Otherwise the sentence may not make sense.

EXAMPLES **Hiking in the Sierra Nevada,** Paulo encountered a mountain lion. [The participle is modified by the prepositional phrase *in the Sierra Nevada.*]
Did you see that lioness **carrying her cubs?** [The participle has an object, *cubs.* The possesive pronoun *her* modifies *cubs.*]
The hiker, **acting quickly,** snapped a picture of the lion. [The participle is modified by the adverb *quickly.*]

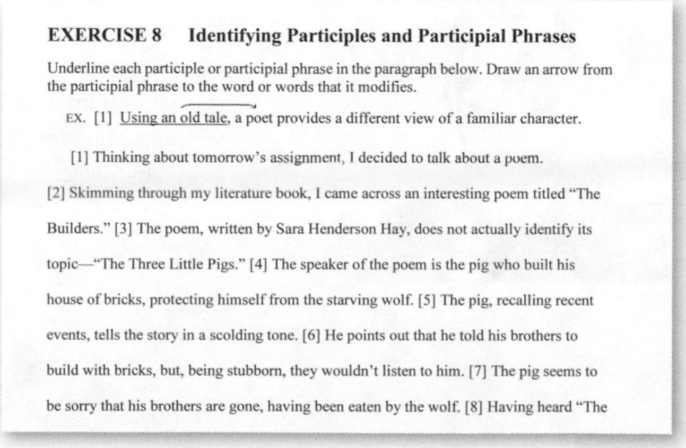

EXERCISE 8 Identifying Participles and Participial Phrases

Underline each participle or participial phrase in the paragraph below. Draw an arrow from the participial phrase to the word or words that it modifies.

EX. [1] Using an old tale, a poet provides a different view of a familiar character.

[1] Thinking about tomorrow's assignment, I decided to talk about a poem. [2] Skimming through my literature book, I came across an interesting poem titled "The Builders." [3] The poem, written by Sara Henderson Hay, does not actually identify its topic—"The Three Little Pigs." [4] The speaker of the poem is the pig who built his house of bricks, protecting himself from the starving wolf. [5] The pig, recalling recent events, tells the story in a scolding tone. [6] He points out that he told his brothers to build with bricks, but, being stubborn, they wouldn't listen to him. [7] The pig seems to be sorry that his brothers are gone, having been eaten by the wolf. [8] Having heard "The

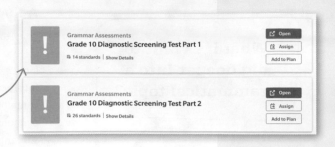
How do I know which grammatical concepts my students need extra help with?

Use the Diagnostic and Summative Assessments

At the beginning of the year, you can use the **Diagnostic Screening Tests**, available on the platform, to get a high-level assessment of student strengths and knowledge gaps in grammatical concepts. It's a multiple-choice test in two parts, each with 50 questions. This will provide you with a great "starting-out point" for the year.

As a part of the full online grammar program, *Into Literature* also contains a full set of **Module Pretests and Summative Test**s. All of the tests are multiple-choice and provide a detailed and comprehensive assessment before and after instruction. Use them before you assign the modules (to assess whether students need the extra help) and after they complete each module (to ensure mastery).

> Grammar Assessments
> **Grade 10 Diagnostic Screening Test Part 1**
> 14 standards | Show Details
> Open | Assign | Add to Plan

> Grammar Assessments
> **Grade 10 Diagnostic Screening Test Part 2**
> 26 standards | Show Details
> Open | Assign | Add to Plan

> Grammar Assessments
> **Grade 10 Module Pretest: Using Pronouns Correctly**
> 22 standards | Show Details
> Open | Assign | Add to Plan

> Grammar Assessments
> **Grade 10 Module Summative Test: Using Pronouns Correctly**
> 22 standards | Show Details
> Open | Assign | Add to Plan

How can I make sure that my students are ready for the writing assessment at the end of the year?

Yes, Students Will Be Scored on Their Language

We know that grammar is a critical part of the ELA curriculum, all year round. But we also know that many students will be held accountable for their mastery of this topic at a critical point of the year: in an end-of-year writing assessment. To help them prepare for this, each end-of-unit task contains an integrated editing lesson focused on a specific grammatical topic. Use these targeted lessons to build students' proficiency in key language skills.

Writing Task

4 **EDIT YOUR ESSAY**

Edit your draft to make sure your essay reflects standard English conventions and spelling.

Ed · Interactive Grammar Lesson: Spelling

Watch Your Language!

SPELL COMMONLY CONFUSED WORDS CORRECTLY

Many pairs of English words are **homophones:** They are pronounced the same way but are spelled differently and have different meanings, like *your* and *you're* and *principal* and *principle*. There are other words that are close in pronunciation but different in spelling and meaning, like *accept* and *except*. This chart includes a few commonly confused words that might appear in an expository essay.

Words	Definitions	Examples
affect/effect	As a verb, *affect* generally means "to influence," but it can also mean "to pretend; to put on falsely." *Effect* is usually used as a noun that means "result or consequence."	Thinking it would **affect** (influence) her audience's impression of her, Chloe **affected** (faked) a British accent. The **effect** (result) was a roar of laughter.
than/then	Use *than* in making comparisons. On all other occasions, use *then*.	I enjoyed this story more **than** that one. **Then**, I read a third one and liked it most of all.
there/their/they're	*There* is the opposite of *here*. *Their* is possessive and means "belonging to them." *They're* is a contraction for "they are."	**There** you are! Will you help Carmen and Melissa get **their** groceries inside? It's pouring rain and **they're** getting soaked!

APPLY TO YOUR DRAFT

Now apply what you've learned to your own work.

1. **Find a list** of commonly confused words. Print or copy it, read it, and circle words to watch for in your writing. Pro tip: many writers have a short list of confusing or hard-to-spell words they always double-check.

2. **Check your essay** against your list and make appropriate corrections.

3. **Exchange drafts** with a peer and review spelling in each other's work.

Ways to Share

Targeting the Areas of Need

What words should my students focus on learning?

Focus on High-Utility Words

In each prose selection, a manageable list of high-utility words have been selected as target vocabulary. Introduce the words before reading, using the **Expand Your Vocabulary** feature to help students assess their own knowledge of the words.

When they see each word in context, students are given a clear, content-appropriate definition and guidance on pronunciation. Following the reading, you can use the vocabulary activity in the **Respond** section to help students practice using the words in writing and discussion.

Expand Your Vocabulary

Put a check mark next to the vocabulary words that you feel comfortable using when speaking or writing.

conceive	☐
detract	☐
resolve	☐
perish	☐

Turn to a partner and talk about the vocabulary words you already know. Then, use as many vocabulary words as you can in a few sentences telling what you know about the Gettysburg Address.

As you read Abraham Lincoln's speech, use the definitions in the side column to learn the vocabulary words you don't already know.

---

conceive
(kən-sēv´) v. to form or develop in the mind; devise.

ANALYZE SEMINAL U.S. DOCUMENTS

Annotate: Mark details in paragraph 1 that introduce two themes often found in seminal

---

1   **F**our score and seven[1] years ago our fathers brought forth on this continent a new nation, **conceived** in liberty and dedicated to the proposition that all men are created equal.

2   Now we are engaged in a great civil war, testing whether that nation, or any nation so conceived and so dedicated, can long endure. We are met on a great battlefield of that war. We have come to dedicate a portion of that field, as a final resting place for those who here gave their lives that that nation might live. It is altogether fitting and proper that we should do this.

How can I teach strategies that support students' own independent vocabulary acquisition?

Provide Instruction on Strategies

Direct instruction for high-frequency words is useful, but students will acquire most of their vocabulary independently. What can you do to ensure that students have the right tools to build their own knowledge? All of our vocabulary instruction in the Student Edition is paired with a vocabulary acquisition strategy that students can deploy as needed. Devote time to these instructional opportunities and assign the **Practice & Apply** activities to reinforce each strategy you've taught.

Vocabulary Strategy
↳ **Multiple-Meaning Words**

Ed
Interactive Vocabulary Lesson: Words with Multiple Meanings

Words that have more than one definition are considered **multiple-meaning words**. To determine a word's appropriate meaning within a text, you need to look for context clues in the words, sentences, and paragraphs that surround it. Look at the word *fitting* in this sentence from the Gettysburg Address:

> It is altogether <u>fitting</u> and proper that we should do this.

The word *fitting* can mean "the act of trying on clothes" or "a small part for a machine." However, the word *proper* is a context clue that tells you that the correct meaning of *fitting* in this sentence is "appropriate."

PRACTICE AND APPLY

Find the following multiple-meaning words in the speech: *engaged* (paragraph 2), *testing* (paragraph 2), *poor* (paragraph 3), *measure* (paragraph 3). Working with a partner, use context clues to determine each word's meaning as it is used in the speech.

1. Determine how the word functions in the sentence. Is it a noun, an adjective, a verb, or an adverb?

2. If the sentence does not provide enough information, read the paragraph in which the word appears and consider the larger context of the speech.

3. Write down your definition.

> **But what about when students are reading with more independence?**

Have Students Track Their Vocabulary

Ideally, students are reading out of class, independently, in subject areas that interest them the most. And that is one of the best times for students to work on mastering unfamiliar words. The **HMH Study Guides** all include Vocabulary Tracker word logs that students can customize to their needs.

If students are reading a novel or longer work of your choice, challenge them to find a certain number of unfamiliar words as they read and log their findings in a chart. For each word, students can include a definition, a sentence using the word, and a picture that exemplifies the word and its meaning.

STUDY GUIDE

The Namesake by Jhumpa Lahiri

VOCABULARY TRACKER

Use the chart below to record unfamiliar terms that you encounter while reading. Choose words that you are likely to use in future reading, writing, and class discussions in this and other classes. Page references will vary depending on the edition of the book you are reading.

Word	Page	Definition from Context	Dictionary Definition	My New Sentence
incessant	19	An incessant sound is probably continuous.	Continuing without interruption	She slept soundly in spite of the incessant beeping of her alarm clock.

> **How can I support students' vocabulary needs regardless of the text I'm teaching in class?**

Use the Interactive Lessons

We know that you have your own texts that you want to teach, based on current events or your sense of what your unique students are interested in. The **Interactive Vocabulary Lessons** are there to support you and your students. The lessons cover the full range of vocabulary strategies, including ample coverage of word roots and affixes.

Analyzing Word Structure

Many words can be broken into smaller parts. These word parts include base words, roots, prefixes, and suffixes.

> Read these points to learn more about word structure.
>
> Base Words ⌄
>
> A **base word** is a word part that by itself is also a word. Other words or word parts can be added to base words to form new words.

Specific Context Clues

Type of Clue	Key Words/Phrases	Example
Definition or restatement of the meaning of the word	or, which is, that is, in other words, also known as, also called	Most chemicals are *toxic*, or **poisonous.**
Example following an unfamiliar word	such as, like, as if, for example, especially, including	*Amphibians*, such as **frogs and salamanders**, live in the pond by our house.
Comparison with a more familiar word or concept	as, like, also, similar to, in the same way, likewise	Like the rest of my *frugal* family, I always **save most of the money I earn.**

Prefixes

A **prefix** is a word part attached to the beginning of a word. Most prefixes come from Greek, Latin, or Old English.

Prefix	Meaning	Example
mal-	bad or wrong	**mal**function
micro-	small or short	**micro**scope
semi-	half	**semi**circle

Incorporating Academic Vocabulary

How can I improve my students' knowledge of academic vocabulary?

Teach Words That Will Make a Difference

Academic vocabulary words (sometimes referred to as Tier 2 words) show up across academic disciplines—math, science, social studies, ELA—in lessons and assessments. For example, at any point in the day students might be asked to "analyze" a poem or a political speech or a graph, but if they're struggling with the meaning of the word *analyze* all of those tasks are going to be more difficult. Some students will come into your class knowing these words and some will pick them up eventually through reading. But research shows that directly teaching these words and reinforcing them with practice provides real gains for students. Every unit of *Into Literature* focuses on a manageable list of topic-appropriate words that students can learn—words that will enrich their writing and speaking.

● Use the **Build Academic Vocabulary** activity within the **Spark Your Learning** feature to introduce the academic vocabulary words for each unit.

Prove It!
Why should people pay attention to what happens in the natural world? Discuss your ideas using one of the Academic Vocabulary words.

Build Academic Vocabulary
You can use these Academic Vocabulary words to write and talk about the topics and themes in the unit. Which of these words do you already feel comfortable using when speaking or writing?

	I can use it!	I understand it.	I'll look it up.
advocate	☐	☐	☐
discrete	☐	☐	☐
domain	☐	☐	☐
enhance	☐	☐	☐
evoke	☐	☐	☐

Writing
↳ **Letter to the Editor**

Write a letter to the editor advocating for a new National Park. Your proposed park may be a real place you have visited or a place you imagine. Your letter should be brief, about 100–200 words long.

● Use a business letter format and formal language for your letter.

● Make a claim. Why does your park merit National Park designation?

● Discuss one or more reasons, using evidence to support your claim.

● Directly address a possible opposing claim.

● Conclude with a specific and logical call to action.

As you write and discuss, be sure to use the Academic Vocabulary words.

| advocate |
| discrete |
| domain |
| enhance |
| evoke |

● Consult the Teacher's Edition notes to help you revisit these words throughout your teaching of the texts in the unit.

● As students complete the **Choices** activities after reading, challenge them to use the academic vocabulary words in their writing, discussions, and presentations.

Academic Vocabulary

Some examples of the academic vocabulary words in *Into Literature* include:

Grade 9	Grade 10
• dimension	• abstract
• enable	• comprise
• generate	• diverse
• integrate	• innovate
• resolve	• perspective

Assessing Student Progress & Mastery

Ⓔ **Ed**

Getting Started

> **How can I get to know my students' skills—both strengths and areas for growth?**

Get to Know Your Students

It's the beginning of the school year, and a sea of unfamiliar faces stares at you expectantly (or cynically!) at the beginning of each class period. Here are some tips for getting to know what skill strengths and challenges your students are bringing to the classroom:

● Use the **HMH Growth Measure**, a short screener administered three times a year, to understand each student's Lexile® level and proficiency with grade-level reading and language skills. This insight, along with information about personal interests, can help you anticipate, plan, and recommend.

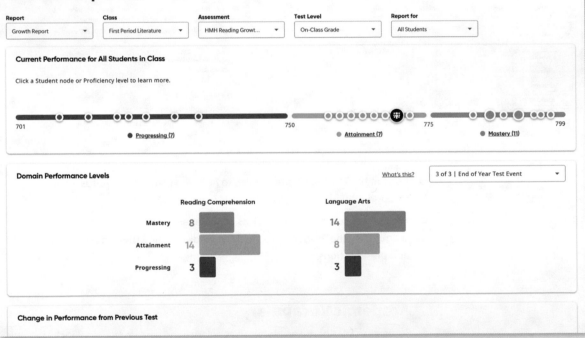

Reports & Insights

Growth Report for All Students

Report	Class	Assessment	Test Level	Report for
Growth Report	First Period Literature	HMH Reading Growt...	On-Class Grade	All Students

Current Performance for All Students in Class

Click a Student node or Proficiency level to learn more.

701   750   775   799

● Progressing (7)   ● Attainment (7)   ● Mastery (11)

Domain Performance Levels   What's this?   3 of 3 | End of Year Test Event

	Reading Comprehension	Language Arts
Mastery	8	14
Attainment	14	8
Progressing	3	3

Change in Performance from Previous Test

● Want more data insights to round out your understanding of each student? Assign the more targeted **Diagnostic Assessments** in reading, grammar, and literature. These assessments are available on our learning platform.

● Don't forget to consult data or feedback from the last academic year. Reach out to the previous grade's teachers to find out whether there are any tips or "look for's" that you should consider as you start the year.

Setting Up Students for Success

How will my students demonstrate comprehension and mastery of skills and standards?

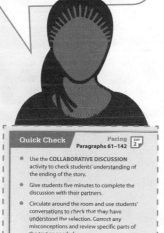

Monitor Progress with Formative Assessments

The embedded formative assessments in the program can help you monitor progress and check understanding. Here are some options:

- Each lesson focuses on one or two reading skills relevant to a particular genre. Use the **Get Ready** feature in the Student Edition to introduce the skills prior to reading.

- Have students apply what they learned by answering the **Guided Reading Questions** in the side margins.

- Reserve five minutes at the end of reading to have students complete the brief **Assessment Practice**. Use a show of hands or polling software to check for understanding.

- After reading, use the **Analyze the Text** questions to guide class discussions and check students' understanding of the skills.

- Use the **Quick Check** notes in the Teacher's Edition to check students' comprehension of the text. The suggestions can help you decide what to do next if students didn't understand the key ideas.

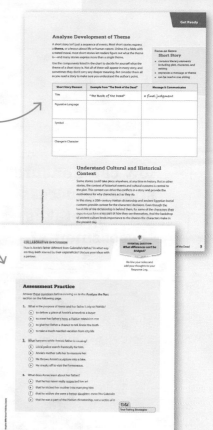

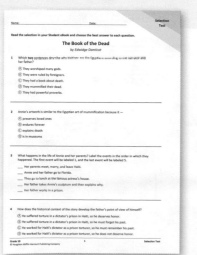

Assess Proficiency with Summative Assessments

Online you will find a library of summative assessments in both editable and interactive formats.

- Use the **Selection Tests** to assess students' mastery of the reading, vocabulary, and language skills taught in each lesson.

- Assign a **Unit Test** to gauge student proficiency with the standards covered in each unit. The **Unit Planning Guides** at the beginning of each unit in your Teacher's Edition show tested skills and standards.

- Customize any assessment to meet your instructional goals. Add, edit, or remove items from online assessments. You can also adjust the editable and printable version of the test.

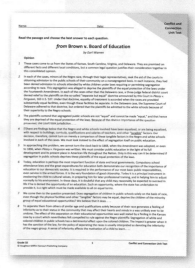

Prepare for High-Stakes Assessments

Like it or not, your students' academic success depends on their performance on high-stakes assessments. The most effective preparation is embedded in daily class instruction and practice. Try these strategies:

- Use the Student Edition as built-in assessment preparation throughout the year. Questions and tasks are modeled after those items on your state assessment and on both the SAT and ACT.

- Look for technology-enhanced items and two-part questions within the Student Edition and on **Selection** and **Unit Tests**.

- Give students ample opportunities to compare and synthesize across texts. The instructional design of the Student Edition and assessments provides plenty of practice.

- Use the **audio excerpts** in Unit Tests to prepare students to sharpen their speaking and listening skills.

- Use the **Writing Task** at the end of each unit to prepare students for the writing portion of your state assessment. Prompts and rubrics provide relevant practice.

- **Ed** The end-of-unit task, along with other prompts that mirror summative writing assessments, are available to assign digitally within **Writable**.

> **How can I ensure student success on high-stakes assessments?**

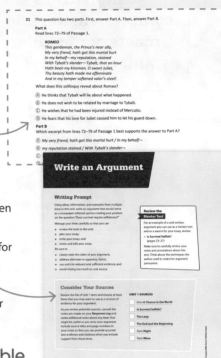

Use Performance-Based Assessments

Students can demonstrate their knowledge of what they learned in many creative ways. Here are some options:

- Assign one or more of the **Choices** activities at the end of each lesson.

- Use the **end-of-unit tasks** in the Student Edition to wrap up each unit. These tasks prompt students to synthesize ideas across texts and share their insights in writing, discussion, debate, or media, for example.

- Consult **Reflect & Extend** pages in the Student Edition for alternate options, including project-based learning opportunities.

> **How else can students demonstrate their knowledge?**

Using Data to Inform Instruction

Learn to Look for Patterns

Into Literature provides a mine of information at your fingertips, so long as you know where and what to look for. Start your investigation on the platform.

How can I use data in my planning and differentiation?

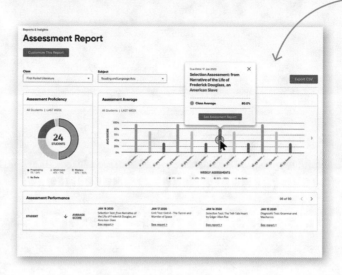

● Consult the **Assessment Report** to see students' overall mastery on all completed assessments. Look at most-missed items and standards before digging in to investigate further.

● View the **Standards Report** to get a sense of each student's cumulative proficiency in different domains and standards. Check back often to help you anticipate when students need more scaffolding or a challenge.

● Check back in on the **Growth Report** to review students' growth in Lexile® and skills over the course of the year.

Adjust Your Plans Accordingly

Use these data insights to anticipate and adapt instruction, or to assign extra practice. Here are some options:

● Browse the **Text Library** for additional titles at the appropriate Lexile® range. The Lexile® filter can help you narrow results.

● Dig deeper into the **Standards Report** and view aligned resources for each standard. Filter by Component to find the resources that will work for your students.

● Use the **Recommend Groups** functionality to see which students need more instruction or practice with the skills taught in a particular lesson.

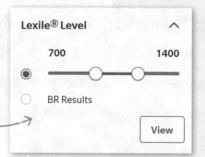

Differentiation

100 Differentiating Instruction for Students Who Struggle

104 Supporting English Learners

108 Infusing Rigor and Challenge

Differentiating Instruction for Students Who Struggle

Identifying the Obstacle

What if I don't know exactly what my students are struggling with?

Tips & Tricks!

Remember that students can excel in one skill set and struggle in another. Rather than labeling students as struggling and successful, try to help each individual draw on strengths and grow where needed.

Use Data, Observation, and Conversation

When students struggle, you'll be better able to help them if you understand their specific obstacles. These tips can help you figure out what those are so you can offer the right support.

- Review the data your district makes available to you.

- **Ed** Analyze the data *Into Literature* provides. If your students have completed the **HMH Growth Measure** and if you've used the learning platform to administer tests, the reports section will be a rich resource. Check the **Standards Report** to see if the student has a pattern of struggling with a particular skill. Use the **Growth Report** to find reading level and proficiency. Both of these reports allow you to compare an individual student's progress to the class average.

- **Ed** Try assigning a **Guided Skills Practice** that is at or slightly below the student's reading level. Use the Lexile® level filter to find one. If the student can master the skill with an easier text, reading level is likely the biggest obstacle, and you can address that.

- Observe and interact with the student. Are there special needs or social and emotional considerations at play? Students often mask learning struggles with challenges or behavioral issues. Talk to them and get to know them better as people.

- Revisit students' records. If they have an IEP or 504, re-read it. Reach out to the students' teams to discuss what supports are recommended and have worked in the past.

Offering the Right Support

What if students aren't understanding the text?

Tips & Tricks!

While you don't always want to group students by reading level, sometimes it's appropriate. A small group can work together to complete a **Text Sketch** or to read an alternative text. If individual students need resources, provide them discreetly at the beginning of class.

Anticipate and Support

Use the **Lesson Planning Guide** in your Teacher's Edition to identify the text complexity of the selection you plan to teach. If you know it will be a challenge for certain students, be ready to offer appropriate supports.

● Use the **Text Support** section of the **Planning Guide** to identify the resources available to you. These might include **Text Sketch**, which provides a high-level visual summary that helps students take notes on key points; **Summary with Targeted Passages**, which provides additional background and easier-to-read summaries of a selection alongside key passages; and **Graphic Organizers** that can help students track events.

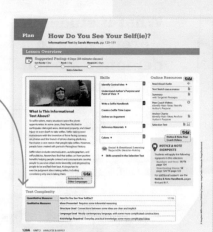

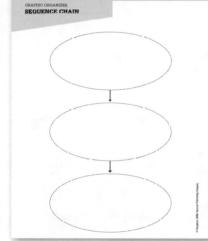

● ⏺**Ed** Decide when to offer each resource. If you want students to begin the lesson with these supports, you can print them out or assign them digitally before the class starts to read. If you want students to engage in productive struggle, wait until after they've done a first read.

● ⏺**Ed** Suggest that students read along with the audio, which is available with read-along highlighting.

● Refer to the **Differentiated Instruction** notes in the Teacher's Edition that are labeled **When Students Struggle**. These focus on potential points of difficulty and provide strategies for supporting comprehension.

● If you know you have students who won't be able to read the selection even with support, try an alternative text. Refer to the **Flexible Short Read Options** in the **Unit Planning Guides** to see the choices. You can also use the Lexile® filter to browse the **Text Library** for texts at an appropriate level.

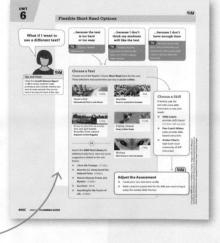

What if students aren't able to demonstrate the skill?

Tips & Tricks!

Find these resources on the Ed platform in the **Intervention, Review, & Extension** section. Use the Component filter to search for what you want.

Review and Remediate

HMH surveyed teachers to identify the skills students struggle with most, and *Into Literature* includes a suite of digital resources that provide additional instruction and practice for these concepts.

- Use the **Skills Support** section of the **Planning Guide** to identify the resources available to you.

- Show or assign **Peer Coach Videos.** These short, stand-alone videos explain key skills and can be shown to the whole class, used as part of a station-rotation model, or viewed by individuals who need a refresher and might benefit from hearing a skill explained by someone else.

- Post or distribute **Anchor Charts.** These colorful summaries of the key skills covered by Peer Coach provide a quick reference for students who need reinforcement.

- Assign **Guided Skills Practice**, so students can practice the skills covered by Peer Coach with texts at the appropriate Lexile® range.

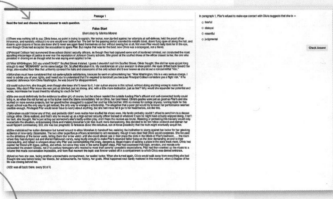

- For more robust remediation, assign **Level Up Tutorials**. Follow up with **Level Up Practice Tests**, so students can demonstrate what they've learned and you can collect data on their progress.

- Enlist the partnership of parents or guardians and any school or after-school staff who work with the students. These resources can be used at home or as part of additional tutoring and instruction.

Managing Differentiation in the Classroom

> **How do I manage having different students doing different things?**

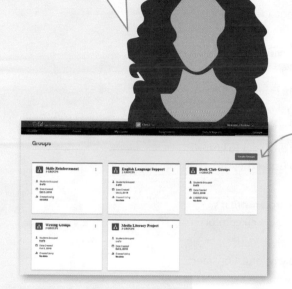

Create Effective Groups and Partnerships

Groups will be your friends. Make sure to mix it up, and bring the class together around the essential themes and for moments of fun to create community.

- **ʘEd** Make targeted assignments. The learning platform allows you to quickly assign appropriate tasks to individuals, groups, or the whole class.

- Group students appropriately. Sometimes, you'll want to group students struggling with the same skill or with the text so that you can give them extra attention while others work more independently. At other times, create mixed groups so that students who have already mastered the skill can provide guidance to those who don't quite get it yet.

- **ʘEd** Use the **Groups** functionality on the learning platform. Ed uses available data to automatically group students based on assessment performance. This allows you to make group assignments easily. Of course, you can also create your own groups based on your insights or preferences.

- After group work, have students share with the whole class. If students have done different readings, they can report on how each one relates to the unit topic or Essential Question, and a larger discussion can follow from there. If they have worked on skills, they can apply the skill to a text the whole class is familiar with.

- Have occasional movement breaks to allow students an outlet for their energy.

- Work in partnership with the students' extended teams, including their grade-level team and their reading coach or other support staff. What struggles transcend your class? What are areas of strength that the students can build from? How can you coordinate your efforts?

- Be mindful that students who struggle will likely not best be helped by additional homework. If you do give practice to be done at home, set clear expectations about time limitations, and keep it under 30 minutes a day.

Supporting English Learners

Planning Your Support

What are some important things to do at the beginning of the year?

Tips & Tricks!

It's a small detail, but taking the extra time to learn and pronounce students' names correctly can go a long way toward making them feel comfortable.

Prepare Routines and Practices

Start off on a positive note by using these tips.

- ☺**Ed** Review any data you have available about the language proficiency level of the students coming into your classroom.

- Determine an approach with any push-in or pull-out teachers who will be available for additional support.

- Make connections with families, and consider whether there are any school resources that you can use to translate materials you might send home to parents or guardians to keep them informed.

- Consider setting up some one-on-one conferences early on to get to know students and create space for them to communicate any issues they are having. Don't assume they will come to you!

- It can be beneficial to invite students' culture into the classroom, but it's important not to push them or put them on the spot. Gauge their comfort level in one-on-one conversations.

- ☺**Ed** Remember that visual reminders can be extremely helpful. Consider posting anchor charts in the room as you cover texts or skills. On the platform, you will find a selection of anchor charts for key literature skills and Notice & Note signposts.

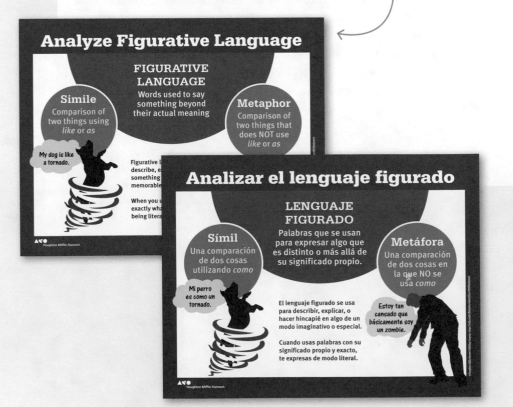

Planning Your Support

What should I be doing at the beginning of the unit?

Entwined
Short Story by **Brian Tobin**

Text Sketch ENG & SPANISH

Summary with Targeted Passages

pp. 198–217   **5** Days   800L

Anticipate the Needs of English Learners

Access planning guides and support resources to meet the needs of all your students.

- Preview the **Unit Planning Guides** to get an overview of texts included in the unit. Note any with a Lexile® level that might challenge your students. Note selections that include **Text Sketch** and **Summaries and Adapted Texts**.

- 🙂**Ed** Access **Spanish Unit Resources** in the Reading Resources category on the platform to find Spanish-language versions of each unit's description and theme, the Response Log, and academic vocabulary.

- 🙂**Ed** Consult the **Multilingual Glossary** to locate any terms for which you want to include additional support in your plan. This resource can be found in the Reading Resources category on the platform and includes a glossary of literary and informational terms, academic vocabulary, and critical vocabulary in ten languages: Spanish, Haitian-Creole, Portuguese, Vietnamese, French, Arabic, Chinese, Russian, Tagalog, and Urdu.

Glossary of Literary and Informational Terms

	English	Spanish
A	**Act** An act is a major division within a play, similar to a chapter in a book. Each act may be further divided into smaller sections, called scenes. Plays can have as many as five acts, or as few as one.	**Acto** Un acto es una división importante dentro de una obra, similar a un capítulo en un libro. Cada acto, a su vez, se puede dividir en secciones más pequeñas, denominadas escenas. Las obras pueden tener hasta cinco actos, o solo uno.
	Alliteration Alliteration is the repetition of consonant sounds at the beginning of words. Note the repetition of the **d** sound in this line: The **d**aring boy **d**ove into the **d**eep sea.	**Aliteración** Aliteración es la reiteración de sonidos consonantes al comienzo de las palabras. Observe la repetición del sonido **d** en esta oración en idioma inglés: The **d**aring boy **d**ove into the **d**eep sea.
	Allusion An allusion is a reference to a famous person, place, event, or work of literature.	**Alusión** Una alusión es una referencia a una persona, un lugar, un acontecimiento o una obra literaria conocidos.

- Incorporate time into your plans to help English learners build background and context for the texts.

- Keep lines of communication open with any push-in or pull-out teachers who may also be supporting these students, so you can align your goals and share resources.

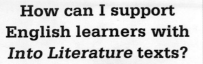

How can I support English learners with *Into Literature* texts?

Tips & Tricks!

Infuse your lesson plans with cooperative learning activities to promote oral language development, grouping students with mixed language proficiency levels. You can use the grouping functionality on the HMH platform to create and manage groups.

Choose the Right Support for Each Text

Into Literature includes a wide selection of support for English learners. Pick and choose what works best for your students.

- ☺Ed Before you introduce any text, use the **Multilingual Glossary** to create a personal word list in the student's native language, or assign it as an activity for students.

- ☺Ed Assign or print **Summaries in Multiple Languages** in English and the student's native language, and bundle them with the following resources to make sure students have a basic understanding of the key ideas, events, and characters in the text:

  - **Summaries and Adapted Texts:** select texts in an adapted format with targeted passages to support less-proficient readers
  - **Text Sketch (in English and in Spanish):** high-level visual summaries of a selection

- ☺Ed Have students use the audio in the eBook to assist with comprehension. They can also turn on the **Read-Along Highlight** feature to track the text as the audio is read.

- Use the Teacher's Edition **Lesson Planning Guides** to find information about the text complexity of each selection and to survey detailed support for that lesson in the **For English Learners** feature, including tips for building background, cultural notes, language objectives, and a list of additional online resources.

- The Teacher's Edition also includes point-of-use **Scaffolding for English Learners** notes to support the teaching of each text.

- Use the oral assessment questions provided with the **Assessment Practice** in each lesson of the Teacher's Edition.

How can I help English Learners access the selection and skills?

For English Learners

Use the **Language Objective** to help students acquire the academic language they need to speak and write about *cause and effect*.

Build Background

Read aloud the title. Point out that *figures* can mean either "numbers" or "people." Explain that this text is about female African American mathematicians who did important work during World War II. Ask what the author meant by *hidden figures*. (*people who were hidden, math done in secret, or both*) Tell students to look for clues to the meaning as they read. Before they read, use the **Text Sketch** in English or Spanish to provide a high-level visual summary of the text.

Cultural Notes

The following words and phrases may be unfamiliar to students:

- *the country that ruled the skies* (paragraph 4): the country that had the most planes and the best ones
- *aircraft industry* (paragraph 5): all the companies that build airplanes
- *"number crunchers"* (paragraph 9): people who do math
- *couldn't satisfy the demand* (paragraph 13): couldn't find enough workers
- *the war effort* (paragraph 18): helping the U.S. do everything possible to win the war

Online Resources ☺Ed

Spanish Resources	Multilingual Glossary
Text Sketch ENG & SPANISH	Summary with Targeted Passages

Scaffolding for English Learners

Language Objective
State one cause and its effect in this selection.

Explain Cause and Effect Explain that history writers often use cause-and-effect organization. The causes are reasons for an action (e.g., the *U.S. joined World War II in 1941*), and the effects are the things that happen because of that action (e.g., *men went to fight; they left jobs open*).

▶ **Substantial** Read aloud paragraphs 12 and 13. Then have students fill in the missing words to identify a cause and its effect: Because there were not enough white _____, the government _____ African Americans.

▶ **Moderate** Read paragraph 17 aloud while students follow along. Point out that the writer uses a cause-and-effect structure in this paragraph. Ask: What caused the workers to put up the bathroom signs? (*African Americans were not allowed to use the same bathrooms as whites in Virginia.*)

▶ **Light** Have pairs work together to review paragraphs 13–18. Ask them to locate and state a cause and an effect of African American mathematicians being hired at the laboratory.

Planning Guide

---

from
Hidden Figures

History Writing by Margot Lee Shetterly

This summary of the history writing excerpt includes targeted passages from the text for you to read on your own.

BACKGROUND
World War II started in 1939 and ended six years later. Before the war, most American women did not work outside the home. When the United States entered the war in 1941, many men left their jobs to join the fight. So, women left their homes to do men's work. During this time, African Americans and white Americans in the South were segregated, or kept apart, in most areas of life, including school and work. This excerpt focuses on the Langley Memorial Aeronautical Laboratory in Virginia. At the Langley lab, engineers designed and tested planes used in the war. An engineer is someone who designs and builds machines.

NOTES

SUMMARY
The author uses a quote from an old newspaper ad, or advertisement, to begin the excerpt. The ad invited women to apply for jobs at the Langley Memorial Aeronautical Laboratory.

TEXT SKETCH

de
Figuras ocultas

Obra histórica de Margot Lee Shetterly

QUIÉNES	CUÁNDO	DÓNDE
Las mujeres matemáticas afroamericanas	Durante la Segunda Guerra Mundial	Langley Memorial Aeronautical Laboratory en Virginia

QUÉ
- Se necesitaban muchas mujeres para trabajos que anteriormente tenían los hombres.
- El gobierno necesitaba construir más aviones para la guerra.
- Se probaban los aviones en Langley, Virginia.
- El laboratorio Langley contrataba a mujeres matemáticas blancas, pero necesitaban más ayuda.
- ¿Qué fue lo que abrió nuevas y emocionantes oportunidades para los afroamericanos durante la guerra?

_____

- ¿Cómo se discriminaba todavía a los matemáticos afroamericanos en Virginia?

Text Support for English Learners

How can I support English learners with *any* grade-level text I teach?

ⓞEd

Literature & Language Arts
Novel Study
Record notes to help you analyze any novel you read.

Title of Novel:
Author:

Setting and Characters

1. The story takes place in

2. The action happens in the past / the present / the future. (write one)

3. Jot down some words or phrases that the writer uses to describe the setting.

4. List the names of the major and minor characters.

Major Characters	Minor Characters

Use Sentence Frames

Sentence frames are a helpful tool to scaffold English learners; such frames allow students to think about what they want to say without the distraction of how to phrase their response. Here are some sentence frames you might use to help English learners analyze and appreciate different genres.

Fiction

- The story takes place in…
- The story is told from the…point of view.
- Three words that describe the main character are…
- The main problem in the story is…
- The author communicates an important message about…
- I would/would not recommend this story to a friend because…

Nonfiction

- The main idea is…
- Three details that support the main idea are…
- In this paragraph, the author is saying…
- The author includes this section because…
- The author wrote this because he or she wanted to…
- I agree/disagree with the author about…because…

Poetry

- The poem is mostly about…
- Three details about the poem's form are…
- One thing I noticed about the speaker of the poem is…
- Three words or phrases that really stand out to me are…
- One tool the poet uses is…to communicate…
- The poem communicates an important message about…using these details:…

ⓞEd

Add Skills Support

For additional skills support, you can pair any text with the following *Into Literature* resources.

- **Peer Coach Videos:** videos of students' peers teaching skills
- **Anchor Charts (in English and Spanish):** high-level visual summaries of skills and ideas
- **Level Up Tutorials:** skills-based remediation lessons for students
- **Skills Coach:** skills instruction and activities that can be applied to any text

Infusing Rigor and Challenge

Meeting the Needs of All Students

> How can I meet the needs of my more advanced students?

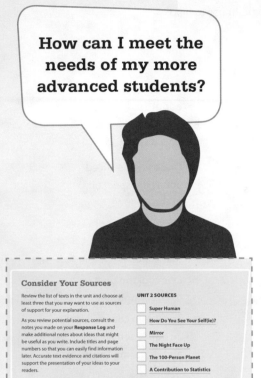

Consider Your Sources

Review the list of texts in the unit and choose at least three that you may want to use as sources of support for your explanation.

As you review potential sources, consult the notes you made on your **Response Log** and make additional notes about ideas that might be useful as you write. Include titles and page numbers so that you can easily find information later. Accurate text evidence and citations will support the presentation of your ideas to your readers.

UNIT 2 SOURCES

- [ ] Super Human
- [ ] How Do You See Your Self(ie)?
- [ ] Mirror
- [ ] The Night Face Up
- [ ] The 100-Person Planet
- [ ] A Contribution to Statistics

Discover Challenge and Rigor at Your Fingertips

Students come into your class with a wide range of experiences and ability levels. As a teacher, you likely spend a lot of time working to get struggling students up to level. But what about students who need a little more rigor and more challenge? With its balanced approach, *Into Literature* has options for your classroom that will allow you infuse rigor and challenges into all of your lessons.

With *Into Literature*, you will find:

- **Rigorous texts:** Our cross-genre units contain a mixture of accessible and challenging texts. You will find short and accessible texts that ease students into the themes and topics, but you will also find classic and complex texts that will push students. To help you decide which texts to teach in a given unit, consult your Teacher's Edition **Lesson Planning Guides** for information about the complexity of each text.

- **Rigorous analysis:** Rich, complex texts are at the heart of *Into Literature*. The instruction and activities all focus on the text. Students are given ample opportunities to make personal connections and to engage in creative work, but they are consistently asked to return to the text for close analysis and study. You can use the **Analyze the Text** questions after each selection to sharpen students' critical thinking, analysis, and synthesis skills. Look in your Teacher's Edition for information about the Depth of Knowledge (DOK) level of each question.

- **Rigorous assignments:** Sometimes, all you need is a short ten-minute assignment to quickly check in on your students. But to get a better sense of how they're performing, you need longer, more complex assignments. The **Choices** activities following each text, as well as the cumulative tasks at the end of each unit, offer opportunities to challenge your students.

Possible responses:

1. **DOK 2:** *Mars is the most Earthlike planet.*

2. **DOK 2:** *The author uses a compare-contrast structure to compare Mars with Earth.*

3. **DOK 3:** *Mars has metal and rock. Settlers could use local dirt to make bricks to build houses. They could use silicon and iron to produce glass and steel for a number of structures, including greenhouses that can be used to grow food. They could use solar energy to produce heat and electricity, and carbon dioxide from the Martian atmosphere to produce methane for fuel for trips to Earth.*

4. **DOK 3:** *The author uses a problem-solution structure in this section to help develop the idea that settling Mars can and should be done. The problem-solution structure explains how settlers could overcome obstacles and problems with the Martian environment to create a habitable settlement.*

5. **DOK 4:** *The numbers and stats help support the idea that building a colony on Mars will be challenging but possible.*

6. **DOK 4:** *Settlers would have a mostly vegan diet because they would be consuming mostly plant-based foods that they might grow on Mars. Students might cite the word colony as one they figured out, based on the word habitat and the last line of the paragraph.*

Meeting the Needs of All Students

☺ Ed

> How can I go beyond just giving students extra work?

☺ Ed

Tips & Tricks!

Remember that on Ed you can browse through all of the selections by Lexile®. This will help you locate and assign a text at the right level of complexity.

Find Flexible Options That Go Beyond Extra Work

Some of your students aren't struggling with on-level work. One of the easiest things to do for those students is to give them … more work. But what if you want to give them different texts or tasks to work on—ones that will challenge them or push them to develop new and useful skills?

Into Literature contains a varied set of extension activities that will help you get beyond handing out extra work.

- **Leveled Texts Library:** Choose from a diverse set of selections that range from easy to very hard. You can choose the selections that you know will appeal to students or choose from the suggested unit-level connections to stay focused on the unit assignments.

- **Novels:** There are lots of ways to incorporate longer texts in your classroom: whole-class instruction, literature circles, or independent work. But however you incorporate them, HMH has a varied set of options to choose from, including classic and contemporary works and texts that will speak to a broad range of experiences and backgrounds. Consult the **Flexible Long Reads** section of the **Unit Planning Guides** in your Teacher's Edition to help you choose appropriate novels for those students who need a challenge. You might also assign some of the **Choices** prompts and activities in the **HMH Study Guides** for these titles.

Media
↳ **Contrast Collage**

Movies and TV shows have often oversimplified the lives of Native Americans. Create a poster or video collage that contrasts media clichés with the range of experiences and reality of Native American lives. Include text or voiceover narration explaining how the clichés fail to represent Native American experiences accurately.

Choose a Text

Choose one of the recommended **Long Reads** for this unit. The books featured here provide additional opportunities for students to explore the Unit 2 theme and Essential Question in depth.

All the Light We Cannot See
Novel by Anthony Doerr

Women in Blue
Nonfiction by Cheryl Mullenbach

Does My Head Look Big in This?
Novel by Randa Abdel-Fattah

- **Independent Reading:** You do a lot of reading with your students. But we all know that the ultimate goal is for students to read with independence, without scaffolds and supports, at the appropriate Lexile® level. The **Reader's Choice** strand is designed to match students with the right texts, including high-complexity options.

- **Media Projects:** Some students need something totally different. How about responding to the unit by writing a song? Or creating a comic strip? Or producing a documentary? Every unit in the program has a suggested **Media Project** for you to choose from, to stretch students or to let them show their creative side. You can find instruction and support for each activity online.

What guidance is there in the Teacher's Edition on rigor and challenge?

Find Ample Support for Stretching Your Students

When you're planning your lessons, one of the many things you're thinking about is the level of rigor you want and how to plan for all of your students, including those above level. Your *Into Literature* Teacher's Edition gives you planning support and point-of-use suggestions that you need.

- **Text Complexity:** You know that text complexity is a complicated thing. Having a Lexile® score is always helpful, but it's impossible to boil the complexity of a text down to a number. That's why every selection contains a full Text Complexity rubric, focusing on what, specifically, makes this text more or less complex.

Text Complexity		
Quantitative Measures	**The Bombing of Black Wall Street**	1140L
Qualitative Measures	**Ideas Presented** Mostly explicit, but with some implied meanings.	
	Structure Used Organization of main ideas and details is complex, but sequential.	
	Language Used Mostly explicit, but historical or cultural allusions are made.	
	Knowledge Required A basic knowledge of American history and culture is expected.	

For Students Who Need a Challenge

How do I support students who need a challenge?

- **To Challenge Students** note on page 448 provides an opportunity for students to extend and enrich their understanding of the text.
- Have students examine how the author uses framing as a narrative technique. Have students identify the two stories in Keyes's article, trace their chronology, and then discuss how the manuscript's discovery affects both the grandson and the reader.

- **Challenging Students:** Every selection in the program contains a planning note (**For Students Who Need a Challenge**) that highlights point-of-use suggestions on what you can do to keep advanced students engaged and developing. It also highlights specific aspects of the lesson that might be well suited for advanced students—for example, a **Choices** activity that might be something to steer advanced students toward.

Cross-Curricular Connection

Research Expressions of Emotion Have students review paragraphs 19–25. With the class, make inferences about the narrator's and Daria's emotions in the passage. (*fear, anxiety, despair*) Tell students that biological and environmental factors influence the ways people experience and express negative emotions such as fear.

- Ask students to compare the ways the narrator and Daria each expressed their emotions in the passage.
- Have partners or small groups research factors that influence the ways people express, experience, and manage negative emotions.

Have students share their findings in a brief class presentation or discussion.

- **Cross-Curricular Resources:** At point of use, you will find suggested **Cross-Curricular Connections**. Reaching across the curriculum to deepen and broaden your students' knowledge is a great way to infuse your classroom with rigor.

Extending Students' Learning

> Beyond the text sets in the program, what other resources does *Into Literature* have for me to use?

Go Beyond the Textbook

Much of the focus of *Into Literature* is on the selections and the support for those selections. In addition, the program offers other engaging and flexible resources you can use to make sure that students are reaching their potential.

- **Interactive Lessons:** On Ed you will find a diverse set of stand-alone lessons on Grammar, Writing, Speaking and Listening, and Vocabulary that you can assign based on the needs of your students. For example, if you have students who want to dig deeper into a writing concept, such as incorporating textual evidence in more sophisticated and varied ways, you can assign them more detailed and granular lessons to get them to the next level.

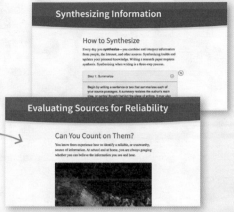

- **Writable** Browse **Writable**'s extensive library for prompts and assignments that you can use to extend students' learning. You might search by skill if you want to provide more practice in a targeted area, or use the rubrics and resources within Writable to create your own assignments.

- **Current Events:** There a world outside your classroom, and bringing that world into your daily lessons is a great way to expand and deepen your students' understanding. Through Ed, you have access to curated Current Events links that are timely, sophisticated, and safe for your classroom.

- **Peer Coach Videos:** *Into Literature* provides a library of videos in which students' peers teach them more about key skills, such as citing text evidence and analyzing themes. How about stretching your students and having them create peer coach videos of their own? Encourage them to choose skills in which they are "experts."

Purposeful Technology

114 Getting the Most Out of
Ed: Your Friend in Learning

120 Integrating Technology
into the ELA Classroom

124 Promoting Digital Literacy

128 Making the Most of an
Accessible Learning Experience

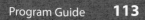

Getting the Most Out of Ed: Your Friend in Learning

Getting Acquainted with Ed

What does the platform offer me?

Tips & Tricks!

New to *Into Literature*? No worries! Start your orientation of the program by exploring the **Professional Learning** section of Ed.

Assignments Overview

Due Today   Total Pending **11**

📖 **Martian Metropolis Text Sketch**   **3** >
   20-21 ELA 104 Sec-1Cervantes

🌐 **Analyze Character**   **0** >
   20-21 ELA 104 Sec 3-Cervantes

📐 **Recognize Text Organization**   **8** >
   20-21 ELA 104 Sec 4-Cervantes

Explore Flexible Resources and Tools at Your Fingertips

Use the HMH learning platform to view the *Into Literature* scope and sequence for your grade level, dip into flexible resources, curate your own lesson plans, create assignments and groups, and monitor student progress.

Into Literature Digital Units and Lessons

- Six thematic units cover a range of grade-appropriate topics and pair high-interest texts with the ELA skills your students need to learn, practice, and progress as readers and writers.

- Access countless resources to create units, lessons, or individual assignments that meet your learning goals.

And So Much More...

- Log in and check your dashboard at least once a week. This will give you an overview of any assignments you need to review, announcements about platform updates, and other helpful messages.

- Track assignments (for the whole class, small groups, or individuals) and monitor students' progress.

- Review assessment results and track student proficiency and growth.

- Create and manage small groups, and easily assign resources to your groups.

- Create your own lesson plans.

- Create custom assessments and test items.

- Find an ever-growing library of professional learning resources from authentic classroom videos, to tips from other teachers and our team of experienced coaches, to support for implementing *Into Literature*.

Available Resources

There are a variety of resource types available for you to use.

- **eBook**: Interactive digital content that launches in the HMH digital reader, and includes read-along audio and highlighting for text selections, annotation tools, **Teacher Review** functionality, and ability to assign to Google® Classroom

- **PDF**: Downloadable and printable resources

- **Digital Assessment:** Diagnostic, formative, and summative tests with interactive items; student assessment data collected and displayed in reports

- **Editable File:** Downloadable, editable, and printable resources

- **Video**: Brief videos for a variety of instructional purposes

- **External Links**: Links to age-appropriate and relevant content, such as current events, that relates to *Into Literature* units

Getting Acquainted with Ed

How do I find what I'm looking for?

Tips & Tricks!

Whether you are browsing lesson lists, standards, or search results, you can use filters to help narrow the results.

Try Five Ways to Locate Resources

Depending on what you are seeking, there are many ways to find the resources you need on the HMH learning platform.

1. Browse the units and lessons in the unit carousel. Select a unit and browse through its various lessons. Click on a lesson to see a list of all the resources related to that lesson.

2. Use these resource categories to browse different resource types.

3. You can also browse by standards. Select the standard you're interested in to see a list of all of the resources associated with that standard.

4. If you are looking for something specific, you can search by keyword.

5. To find what you're looking for, refer to the **Resource Overview**, which is located in the Program Overview category on the platform. Keep in mind that the content on Ed is always evolving—in response to feedback from users like you! Check the Help section to learn about the latest ways to browse and explore resources.

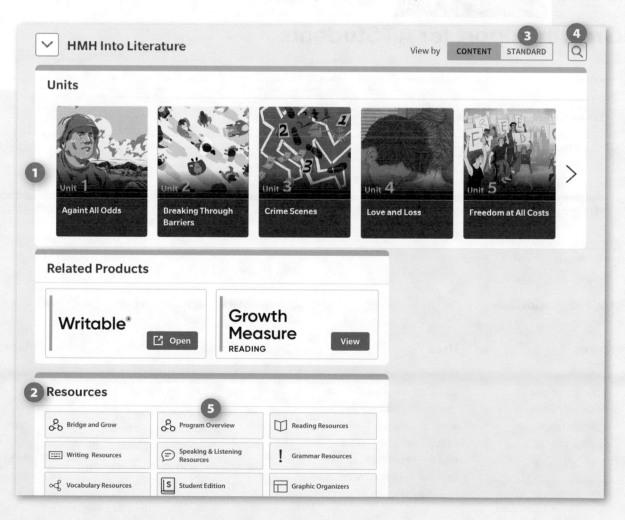

Let the Data Guide Your Choices

Data and reports can help you monitor students' progress and make teaching decisions that support the needs of all your students.

What do I do with all these reports?

Growth Report

Features

- Administer the **HMH Growth Measure** three times a year: beginning, midpoint, and end
- Use the results to identify each student's Lexile® range, proficiency in reading comprehension and language domains, and growth across various increments of the year

Uses

Use this report to identify students at risk, and to benchmark their performance. You can also use the Lexile® scores to help you gauge when a text will be too hard or too easy for your class and to differentiate.

Growth Report for All Students

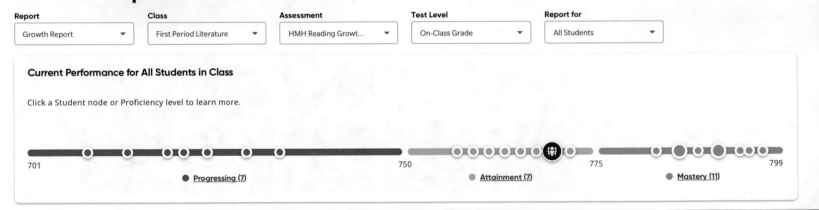

Report
Growth Report

Class
First Period Literature

Assessment
HMH Reading Growt...

Test Level
On-Class Grade

Report for
All Students

Current Performance for All Students in Class

Click a Student node or Proficiency level to learn more.

701   750   775   799

● Progressing (7)   ● Attainment (7)   ● Mastery (11)

Standards Report

Features

- Cumulative representation of students' performance against standards throughout the year
- Links to resources related to each standard

Uses

Use this report to check students' progress against standards and identify areas of concern. Refer to the aligned resources to find the teaching materials that will help you meet their needs.

Assessment Report

Features

- Shows overall class performance on program assessments
- Includes overall scores, class proficiency bands, and troublesome items and standards
- Allows for in-depth item analysis across the class or by student

Uses

Gauge how students performed on the selection or unit and identify skills you might want to reteach. Pivot from this report to planning your next whole-class lesson or unit, or plan some targeted differentiation for individual students or groups.

Making Ed Work for You

> **What if I don't want to teach what you've suggested?**

☺️ **Ed**

Tips & Tricks!

Not only can you create your own lesson plans; you can also use the HMH platform to share them with your fellow teachers.

Make It Your Own

Into Literature was created with your need for flexibility in mind. Whether you want to adapt the scope and sequence, or start from scratch and create your own curriculum, or anything in between, HMH has got you covered.

Fine-Tuning

- If you are looking to fine-tune a lesson we have provided, begin by creating your own lesson plan on the platform.

- Select the unit and lesson you'd like to fine tune from the program carousel. Preview the resources included with this lesson—you might start with the **Lesson Planning Guide** in the Teacher's Edition so you can scan our suggested approach.

- As you make decisions about which portions of the lesson to include, add them to your custom lesson plan. For example, you may decide not to teach the language convention skill we've paired with the text, so you can omit those related resources from your plan.

- You can browse across all the *Into Literature* resources and add additional supporting resources to meet different learning goals. For example, you might decide to replace our suggested literary skill with a different one. In this case, you may choose to add a **Peer Coach Video**, **Anchor Chart**, and **Skills Coach** for the skill you have selected. As you find additional resources, add them to your custom plan.

Starting From Scratch

- If you are looking to create your own lesson from scratch, begin by creating your own lesson plan on the platform.

- If you have hyperlinks to external resources, you can include them in the **Plan Description.**

- Browse for the resources you'd like to use to build your lesson.

- As you find resources you'd like to include, add them to your plan.

What are the benefits of assigning the readings digitally?

Use Audio Support and Annotation Tools

There are some benefits to assigning readings digitally:

● When reading an HMH eBook in our digital reader, students can access the read-aloud selection audio and hear the text read aloud to them. The digital reader also includes a read-along highlighting feature, which highlights the text as it is read aloud so students can easily follow along with the audio.

● As they read, students can annotate the text digitally, and you can review their annotations from your own copy of the digital assignment by using the **Teacher Review** functionality.

● Working in the digital text allows you to easily present the text to the whole class for discussion purposes, and display either your own text annotations or samples of students' annotations.

ⓒ Ed

Tips & Tricks!

Students can download an app to access digital readings offline anytime, anywhere.

Read: from Narrative of the Life of Frederick Douglass

Contents | Play Audio Review Notes More

Class 1 ✕

‹ Gerlach, Wilfrid ✕ ›

🔍 Search

Select All to Print ☐

˅ Analyze & Apply [4]

☑ Gerlach, Wilfrid ☐

I was now about twelve years old, and the thought of being a slave for life began to bear heavily upon my heart.

🕐 June 15 2020, 10:24am

This would be a good jumping off point for a thesis sentence for my essay. What would this have felt like? How might I have dealt with this situation and these emotions?

View on Page

☑ Gerlach, Wilfrid ☐

The moral which I gained from the dialogue was the power of truth over the conscience of even a slaveholder.

5 I was now about twelve years old, and the thought of being *a slave for life* began to bear heavily upon my heart. Just about [this time I] of a book entitled "The Columbian Orator." [Every opportunity I] got, I used to read this book. Among much [of other interesting] matter, I found in it a dialogue between a [master and his slave]. The slave was represented as having run [away from his master] three times. The dialogue represented [the conversation wh]ich took place between them, when the slave was retaken the third time. In this dialogue, the whole argument in behalf of slavery was brought forward by the master, all of which was disposed of by the slave. The slave was made to say some very smart as well as impressive things in reply to his master—things which had the desired though [unexpected effect; for the conversation resulted in the]

This would be a good jumping off point for a thesis sentence for my essay. What would this have felt like? How might I have dealt with this situation and these emotions?

View in Panel | Save and Close

Making Ed Work for You

How will I review students' digital work?

Use Assignments, Teacher Review, and Reports

Ed offers a variety of ways to monitor students' work and progress, depending on the kind of assignment you have created.

● Review your assignments in the Assignment List, and track students' progress. From this list, selecting an eBook assignment or assessment will allow you to launch and review students' work.

● Launch eBook assignments in the HMH digital reader to review how students have interacted with the text. Select the **Teacher Review** functionality from the top navigation bar and select students whose work you'd like to review. You can also use the feedback icon on the eBook page to leave feedback for students.

Feedback

Feedback for: Rose, Marlowe
Assignment: Student Edition: Respond: Analyze the Text

Type feedback here...

Send

Respond: Analyze the Text

Respond

Analyze the Text

Support your responses with evidence from the text.

Review what you **noticed and noted** as you read the text. Your annotations can help you answer these questions.

Infer

Class 1

Gerlach, Wilfrid

Search

Select All to Print

Analyze & Apply   4

Gerlach, Wilfrid

Now this is the point. You fancy me mad.

June 15 2020, 2:58pm

Interesting how the narrator is talking directly to the audience and pleading his case to us.

View on Page

● If you have created online writing assignments, you can easily review students' writing progress, scan peer feedback, and provide feedback of your own.

● Use the reports on Ed to monitor progress on assessments.

What if I would rather print resources rather than manage assignments digitally?

Use Our Printable Resources

If you prefer to assign and manage student work in the physical world, you can limit your platform use to locating resources—there is so much to print out!

● Any of our PDF resources can be easily printed. They include a variety of practice activities, graphic organizers, and text and skills support.

● Use the **Text Library** to find printable texts across genres and Lexile® levels.

● If you prefer not to assign digital assessments, you can print out **Selection Tests** and **Unit Tests** and have students respond on paper.

Integrating Technology into the ELA Classroom

Getting Started

> **What advice do you have for those of us who are new to teaching with technology?**

Start With Your Learning Objectives

HMH Into Literature consultant Weston Kieschnick acknowledges that we've collectively gotten caught up in buzzwords and technology tools at the expense of purposeful pedagogy and instruction. When it comes to successfully implementing technology in your classroom, begin with the basics—what you want your students to achieve.

- **Reflect on and outline your instructional objectives.** Is it your goal to model close reading and annotation? To determine which students need more support? To promote peer collaboration in writing and revision? Let your learning objectives drive your use of digital tools, not the other way around.

- **Choose a digital tool.** From polling software to vocabulary game applications to collaborative writing and presentation tools, there are just-right tools for whatever you are trying to do. Look no further than the pages in this article for some suggestions.

> *"Technology is awesome. Teachers are better."*
>
> "We have to layer technologies onto our instruction . . . we must do so with strategy, pedagogy, and purpose. That comes from educators, not from the technologies themselves."
>
> — from *Bold School: Old School Wisdom + New School Technologies*

Weston Kieschnick

- **Lean on the support and guidance of fellow educators.** Remember that you are not in this alone. Pose questions on social media or in your professional learning community and you'll soon see the tips and guidance pour in. Enlist the support and advice of your school technology coordinator, and be open to experimenting with new ideas and approaches. Don't be afraid to embrace them! Even if a new tool turns out to be an "epic fail," it's still a learning opportunity.

Enhancing Whole-Class Instruction

How might I use technology in whole-class instruction?

Consider the Options

Technology can ignite your whole-class instruction, as well as adding interest and variety to your lessons. Depending on your instructional objectives, here are some ideas you might consider.

If you want to...   *Try This!*   *Using These Tools*

If you want to...	Try This!	Using These Tools
☑ Generate Class Discussion	Create a digital poll that invites students to share their opinions about an Essential Question or an argument. (Example: What does it take to survive a crisis?) Use the results to guide a meaningful class discussion at the beginning of a unit.	* Google® Forms * SurveyMonkey®
☑ Gauge Understanding or Mastery	A three-question **Assessment Practice** follows each text in *Into Literature*. While you can assign this resource as independent practice on our platform, you also might consider using a whole-class quiz site to quickly learn which students did not comprehend the main ideas.	* Quizlet® * Google® Forms
☑ Expand Students' Vocabulary	Incite friendly competition among students by creating a game that tests their knowledge of unit academic and lesson vocabulary words.	* KAHOOT!® * Vocabulary.com * Gimkit
☑ Model Close Reading	Project the teacher's version of the **Student eBook** and use the highlighter and notes to annotate the text and answer questions. Thinking aloud about the process of close reading can help your students see how it's done.	* Student eBook on ☺Ed
☑ Allow More Class Time for Meaningful Discussion, Group Work, or Writing	Try a blended-learning approach to maximize valuable class time. Create a video or screen capture of yourself delivering instruction and have students review that lesson at home. Use class time for discussion, questions, and small-group differentiation.	* Apple QuickTime * Screencastify
☑ Increase Student Autonomy	Challenge your students to be teachers for a day! Invite groups of students to instruct the rest of the class in a particular skill. Allow students to use presentation software to illustrate or emphasize key points.	* Microsoft Powerpoint * NearPod * Google® Slides

☺Ed

Tips & Tricks!

Have students annotate the text as homework or independent practice. Then, use the Teacher Review function in your eBook to project students' annotations in your next day's lesson.

> How can I use technology in small-group and independent work?

Analyze Author's Purpose

To figure out how authors achieve their purpose, think about:

How did the author convince me to agree with her?

TEXT STRUCTURE
What did it highlight?

Example: A problem/solution structure can highlight the author's ideas.

TONE
How did it affect the way you connected with the message?

Example: An outraged tone might make people want to take action.

TOOLS AND TECHNIQUES
How did the appeals, language, or graphics contribute to the message?

Example: Appeals to emotion might make an audience agree with the author.

Have a Plan

If you establish a plan and set up your classroom ahead of time, you can use technology in instructionally meaningful ways to support small-group and independent practice. This allows you to spend your time differentiating instruction for those students who need it most.

Implement these ideas to keep the rest of the class on track.

Use Station Rotations

- **To Reinforce Skills** Have groups of students review a **Peer Coach** video and accompanying **Anchor Chart** for a particular skill you've taught recently. To practice the skill, you might have the group work through a **Level Up Tutorial**.

- **To Inspire Signpost Discussions** Assign small groups of students to read a text of their choosing and ask them to look for Notice & Note signposts. Encourage them to use their eBook annotation tools to highlight and identify those signposts, as well as to discuss the anchor question.

Assign Independent Practice

- **For More Skills Application** Assign **Guided Skills Practice** for on-level skills practice.

- **For Reading Support** Have students listen to the read-aloud of a particular text. You may want to encourage them to turn on **Read-Along Highlighting** so that they can better follow along.

- **For Improving Writing** Use the Peer Review feature in **Writable** to inspire collaboration and revision in your classroom. Set it up so that each student reviews the work of two or three classmates.

Writable

Create Project-Based Learning Opportunities

Use the **Media Projects** at the end of each unit to kickstart small-group project-based learning. From Google® Slides to Nearpod to GarageBand to iMovie, there is no shortage of digital tools to inspire students' creativity. Encourage groups to start low-tech or no-tech: planning and storyboarding are even more important than the final product.

Create a Movie Trailer

MEDIA PROJECTS

Create a Movie Trailer

This unit explores epic journeys, including Homer's *The Odyssey*. What would a modern odyssey be like? Create a trailer for a movie about a modern quest that includes onscreen text, images or video footage, and music.

Now Go Create!

ⓔ *Ed*

Teaching Remotely

> **How do I set up my class for successful distance learning?**

Stay Connected

If recent events have taught us anything, it's that sometimes we have to be ready to teach and learn at a distance. Yet, with a little preparation, patience, and perseverance, we can use technology to keep classrooms connected. These tips can help with virtual routines.

Get Ready for Your Close-Ups

● Remote learning can be isolating for educators and students alike. Maintain your connections via video. Video-conferencing applications like Google® Hangouts, Microsoft Teams, and Zoom® can help to cultivate a classroom community. Use the **Virtual Classroom** function on our platform to manage your classroom collaboration.

● Work with your administration on the setup and logistics, and then experiment with the application prior to use. Consider doing a dry run with a colleague before showtime!

● If you don't have video conferencing as an option, record and post a video of yourself each day. You might preview the day's assignments or deliver a short lesson.

● Not all students will have access. Ensure that video sessions are optional, and make an extra effort to follow up—either by email or telephone—with those students who can't connect. Take advantage of the offline app so that students can access *Into Literature* digital resources without an Internet connection.

Subject-Verb Agreement

Subject-Verb Agreement

A verb should agree with its subject in number.

OBJECTIVES
• Identify verbs that agree in number with their subjects.

Singular subjects take singular verbs.

EXAMPLE
The peach *seems* ripe.
[The singular verb *seems* agrees with the singular subject *peach*.]

WHY IT MATTERS
Errors in subject-verb agreement can distract your audience from your message, no matter how powerful it is.

Balance Real-Time Teaching with Independent Work

● Strive for real-time learning each day even for a short time. You might review vocabulary or literary and informational text terms using some of the game applications on page 121. Another option is to model close reading of part of a text before having students complete the reading independently. Hold a class discussion about the rest of the text in a subsequent video session.

● Assign independent reading each day, having students use the read-along highlighting function in their eBooks.

● Browse through the digital lessons on writing, speaking and listening, vocabulary, and grammar, which are perfect for self-guided independent work.

● Consider having students post a video doing a close-reading of an excerpt from a text. Students can consult the **Close Read Screencasts** as models and use screen-capture software to produce their final product.

Chorus. Two households, both alike in dignity,
In fair Verona, where we lay our scene,
From ancient grudge break to new mutiny,
Where civil blood makes civil hands unclean.
From forth the fatal loins of these two foes,
A pair of star-crossed lovers take their life,
Whose misadventured piteous overthrows
Doth with their death bury their parents' strife.
The fearful passage of their death-marked love,
And the continuance of their parents' rage,
Which, but their children's end, naught could remove,
Is now the two hours' traffic of our stage,

• Civil means "involving ordinary citizens."
• Civil also means "polite."

Communicate Regularly

● Let students and parents know that you are available by email or chat during school hours each day.

● Consider hosting office hours for parents each week. Remember—most parents are not experts at supervising learning at home and may appreciate your tips and tricks. Your reassurance may just assuage some anxiety at home!

Promoting Digital Literacy

Understanding the Basics

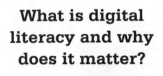

> **What is digital literacy and why does it matter?**

Create Critical Thinkers, Consumers, and Citizens

Never have we had more information and entertainment at our fingertips.

- Social-media influencers feature brands and products in their videos. We are subtly persuaded to buy.

- The 24/7 news cycle captures our attention with the latest headlines and commentary. That news shapes our perceptions of the world.

- Movie studios release their latest films, hoping for box-office blockbusters. We flock to the theaters to escape reality and be entertained.

John Naisbitt, who co-wrote the now decades-old book *Megatrends*, said that "We are drowning in information but starved for knowledge." Never has this statement been truer than in today's world. The *quantity* of information has exploded because anyone can publish content. Yet, in some cases, *quality* has diminished. With fewer checks and balances on that content, it's hard for us to know what to believe, whom to trust, and how such media messages affect our purchasing decisions, political opinions, beliefs, and perceptions.

This is a strong case for **media literacy**—the ability to read, analyze, evaluate, and think critically about the media messages students are exposed to each day. Media literacy also involves students' ability to produce messages for specific purposes and audiences, using the techniques they've learned about in their analysis. Media-literacy education belongs in the ELA classroom.

Types of Media Messages

Exploring Key Questions

How can I help students analyze media messages?

Introduce and Discuss Five Questions

Leaders in media-literacy education agree on five key questions for analyzing any media message, be it a political ad, social-networking site, commercial, movie, or news blog. At the beginning of the year, introduce these questions to your students, using the information in the chart. Revisit these questions throughout the year as part of any media lesson you use in specific units of study.

Five Key Questions	Why They're Important
1 Who created this message?	Media messages can come from a variety of sources—for example, individuals spouting strong opinions, companies selling products, or filmmakers weaving imaginative stories. Identifying the creator of a media message is the first step in understanding its purpose and techniques.
2 What techniques are used to grab and hold my attention?	Bold colors and eye-catching logos can emphasize key benefits of a product. Lighting, sound effects, and editing can draw us into a suspenseful movie scene. Sensational headlines can skew our understanding of an unfolding news story. Analyzing these techniques can make us more aware of how they affect our decisions, actions, and perceptions.
3 How might different people understand this message differently?	No two people will experience a media message the same way. That's because age, gender, race, values, lifestyle, and opinions influence what people see and hear. For instance, a victim of identity theft will have a different reaction to a movie about the topic than someone who has never experienced it firsthand. When analyzing any media message, consider how your own experiences are influencing you and think about how others might respond.
4 What values, lifestyles, and points of view are reflected in—or omitted from—this message?	All media messages are constructed. Just as creators make choices about information to include and techniques to use, they are just as deliberate about what to leave out. Through these choices, creators transmit particular viewpoints and values. Ask: What ideas are being "sold"? What values and behaviors are portrayed in a positive light? In a negative light? Consider the ways in which the media message influences your worldview.
5 Why is this message being sent?	In simplistic terms, the purpose of any media message is to inform, entertain, and/or persuade. Yet, it's important for audiences to uncover deeper motives. Most media messages are created to gain profit or power. Behind every amusing social-media influencer video are sponsors who have paid to feature their products there. Behind every blockbuster film are movie-studio executives hoping for record ticket sales. Consider both overt and subtle purposes when examining any message.

How can I incorporate media analysis into the study of literature?

Sound Elements

Music and Sound Effects	Sounds from nature and music can work to build a particular mood that affects the emotional response of the viewer.
Voice-over Narration	Word choices can appeal to viewer emotions, but so can the speaker's vocal expression, emphasis, and pace.

Visual Elements

Images	Art, photos, animation, graphs, and video can work together to share information and create emotional appeal.
Words	Onscreen text in the form of titles, subtitles, captions, or visual guides to the narration can emphasize key ideas.
Juxtaposition	Sequencing shots implies a connection between ideas or events, adding meaning in ways that enhance the message.

Help Students "Read" Media Messages

Like novels, short stories, and nonfiction, media messages are texts worthy of careful study and analysis. Whereas writers employ techniques like foreshadowing, figurative language, and rhetorical devices to craft their texts, media creators use techniques of their own to influence audiences.

The English language arts classroom is the perfect place to make a natural connection between writers' and media creators' crafts. Here are some suggestions you might try.

- **Include media texts in your units of study.** The *Into Literature* Student Edition includes media texts—such as graphic novels, posters, videos, screenplays, and documentaries—embedded within certain units. Take advantage of these built-in opportunities for media analysis.

- **Encourage close viewing.** Like written texts, media texts require multiple viewings. If you are watching something as a class, encourage students to view it first for comprehension and enjoyment. Then watch the clip a second time, pausing periodically to ask questions, discuss techniques, and think critically about purpose and audience.

- **Teach visual techniques.** Different **camera shots** can establish setting, provide key details, or reveal emotion. **Editing** techniques can create fast-paced suspense or communicate a more relaxed mood. **Type**, **font**, and **composition** can convey meaning in each frame of a graphic novel. Make sure students understand the varied visual techniques that media creators have at their disposal. Use the media lessons in the Student Edition to bolster your instruction.

- **Analyze the influence of sound. Voice-over narration** can communicate information and establish a tone of authority in news reports and documentaries. **Music** and **sound effects** can create a mood or influence an audience's emotions. When students "read" media messages, prompt them to consider the effects of specific sounds.

- **Revisit the five questions.** With any media message you teach, refer back to the five questions on the previous page. You'll notice that your students will start to think more critically about what they see and hear through frequent discussions about these questions.

A bully terrorizes a small town until they decide they've had enough.

Bully

Ed

Podcast

Listen to "**Bully**" in your ebook.

Podcast by **Radiotopia/PRX**

from

Maus

Graphic Memoir by **Art Spiegelman**

Cats and mice represent Nazis and Jews in this graphic novel about the Holocaust.

Evaluating Sources

Ⓔd

What are the best ways to teach students to evaluate sources?

Provide Ample Practice

Anyone with media-production skills and inexpensive applications can create content and make it available on the Web for mass consumption. Sometimes, the polish and production value of those sources of content can mask inaccuracies and biases. Being able to evaluate sources critically is an essential skill for college, careers, and, well, life in general! Use these tips to help students practice this essential skill.

- Use the **Interactive Writing Lessons** on evaluating sources to cover the basics as a whole class. For application, look for research-based **Choices** activities following each lesson.

- Make good use of the end-of-unit writing task focused on research. Consider using **Writable** so that students can complete their drafts digitally and take advantage of tools like peer review.

- Check out the **Current Events** category on Ed, which includes access to HMH's own frequently updated site. Browse for up-to-the-minute articles that you might assign to give students practice in evaluating sources.

Creating a Culture of Media Makers

Make the Time for Media Production

Production is a necessary aspect of media-literacy education. It deserves class time in proportion to its instructional weight. Consider these ideas and resources as you work to unleash students' inner creativity.

How can I incorporate media production into my classroom?

- Consult the **Choices** feature after each lesson for activities focused on media production.

- Ⓔd Try out project-based learning! Explore the end-of-unit **Media Projects** on Ed and think about allowing students to demonstrate their knowledge of at least one unit by completing one of these projects.

- Hold a student showcase. Build in time for students to share their final products with the rest of the class.

- Encourage reflection. After each project, ask: What are you most proud of? What would you do differently next time? What was your group's biggest challenge?

Making the Most of an Accessible Learning Experience

Understanding the Basics

Level the Playing Field for Learning

Accessibility is about the right to *equity* for the disabled. Federal law calls for all public schools to offer equity in education to every student they serve. So, providers of instructional materials strive to produce print and digital learning experiences that are usable by all students, regardless of disability.

But approaching something as many-sided as equity in education takes more than minimum compliance to the law or to accessibility guidelines. Beyond compliance, leveling the playing field for learning means instructional design that teaches effectively no matter what method a student uses to perceive it, whether via a screen reader or with closed captioning, whether using special fonts on a large monitor or using Braille.

To create effective learning for a diversity of students, *Into Literature* was designed using **Universal Design for Learning (UDL)** principles. UDL is a science-based framework developed by the Center for Applied Special Technology (CAST), a non-profit organization. UDL offers guidance for "improv[ing] and optimiz[ing] teaching and learning for all people based on scientific insights into how humans learn."

Into Literature was built with these principles in mind. As you review or use the program, ask yourself the questions in the chart. You'll discover that, through UDL and accessibility, *Into Literature* offers all students an equal opportunity to learn.

> **What is accessibility and why does it matter?**

UNIVERSAL DESIGN FOR LEARNING FRAMEWORK

Provide Multiple Means of Engagement	Provide Multiple Means of Representation	Provide Multiple Means of Action and Expression
• Are there choices and autonomy for individual learners?	• Are there ways of customizing how the information is displayed?	• Are students encouraged to use multiple means of expression to demonstrate their knowledge?
• Is the content culturally relevant?	• Are there alternatives for both visual and auditory information?	• Are digital experiences optimized for assistive technology?
• Does the learning experience foster collaboration and community?	• Is vocabulary defined and explained?	• Are there graphic organizers, note-taking devices, and checklists in place to help students manage and comprehend information?
• Are there built-in opportunities for self-reflection?	• Are concepts illustrated through multiple media, not just text?	
• Are assessments accompanied by meaningful feedback?	• Is background information supplied, when necessary?	

Supporting All Learners

How does the *Into Literature* digital experience support all learners?

We Provide Accessible Formats

Into Literature is accessible. Students can use assistive technology, such as screen readers, to perceive and operate core digital materials. Large-type and Braille print publications for students are available through district request processes from the National Instructional Materials Access Center (NIMAC). Beyond the accessibility of core content for students, all users of assistive technology will find a friend in Ed, HMH's digital platform.

Here are some other digital capabilities of *Into Literature* to explore as you consider the diversity of learners in your classroom.

Feature	Benefits
Audio Support	All texts in the eBook include read-aloud audio, with human readers modeling fluency and expression. While some students may use this audio as an accommodation, this feature can help everyone strengthen reading comprehension. The **Read-Along Highlight** feature supports students in tracking their place more easily.
Display and Magnification Support	Most student components within *Into Literature* have dynamic layouts that respond to different device sizes in both landscape and portrait orientations. Not only will all students be able to read comfortably across devices, but students who rely on magnification and zooming will find the support they need. Encourage students to use the zoom function native to their browsers to magnify the content according to their reading needs or preferences.
Annotation and Note-Taking Tools	All student eBooks come with colorful highlighters, an underlining feature, bookmarks, and a self-organizing notebook. Marking up text while reading can help students comprehend story events and main ideas, track unfamiliar words, record evidence, and remember key details for writing and discussion.
Closed Captioning for Videos	**Peer Coach**, **Stream to Start**, and **Media Texts** have closed captioned videos. Closed captioning not only supports hearing-impaired students, but also supports those who prefer reading to listening, as well as anyone teaching or learning in a lively classroom where it might be hard to hear.

Bradbury creates an eerie mood.

View in Panel   Edit Note

Tips & Tricks!

Model close reading using the **annotations tools**. For example, you might have students choose one color for unfamiliar words and one color for author's craft. Invite them to jot down their questions and reactions to the text in their notes.

What accessibility options are available with *Into Literature* assessments?

Understand the Options

The **Diagnostic**, **Selection**, **Unit**, **Book Tests**, and **Guided Skills Practice** banks that come with *Into Literature* are not time-based, as timed assessments can be challenging for many learners who require accommodations. If you plan to use the digital tests on the platform to assess your students, take the time to acquaint them with the various accessibility options. If you decide to use the platform to create your own assessments, keep these suggestions in mind.

When students are taking an assessment, they can . . .

- use the **Accessibility Options** menu to change the color contrast and the font size, as well as exploring the options for zooming in and out on each item.

- use the **Response Masking** feature to help them narrow their choices and eliminate visual distraction.

⬚ Full Screen   1 of 4   ● Accessibility

Passage 1

Read the text and choose the best answer to each question.

Some devices recognize your face. Is that a good thing?

Argument by Kathryn Hulick

(1) You pick up your phone and stare at it. Instantly, the screen unlocks. But it won't do that for anyone else. The phone knows who you are. It recognizes the shape of your face.

(2) Welcome to the world of the latest iPhone. It comes with a feature called Face ID. Apple executive Phil Schiller described it this way at the product launch: "With the iPhone X, your iPhone is locked until you look at it and it recognizes you. Nothing has ever been more simple, natural, and effortless."

(3) Your face isn't the only characteristic you can use as a password. Many smartphones already accept fingerprint logins. Other security systems check the shape of the ear, patterns in the eye, or the way a person walks. All of these characteristics, called biometrics, are unique enough to identify someone.

The author most likely included the information in paragraphs 1–3 to —

○ make an argument against the use of biometrics

○ provide background on the topic of the argument

○ emphasize the security of biometric technology

○ detail strengths of different types of passwords

[Check Answer]

◄ | **1** | 2 | 3 | 4 | Next ►

⬚ Response Masking   ☺Ed

Tips & Tricks!

At the beginning of the year, model how to use the accessibility features in Ed before assigning any digital assessments. In particular, demonstrate how to use the **Response Masking** feature to help with answering questions.

Accessibility options   ✕

Color scheme   Font size   Zoom

Change the background and foreground colors of your activity.

⦿ Black on white (default)

○ Grey on light grey

○ Purple on light green

○ Black on violet

○ Yellow on navy

○ White on black

[Cancel]   [OK]

When creating your own digital assessments, you can . . .

- consider reducing the number of distractors to make the choices more manageable for students.

- make sure that distractors are all distinct from one another and that there is one clear correct answer.

- model each digital item type as a whole class to make sure that the mechanics of answering the item are not a barrier to demonstrating understanding of the learning objective.

- write directions that are simple and clear. There should be no confusion about the task students are required to complete.

- think about whether you can assess the same learning objectives in different ways, such as with a performance assessment, rather than with a multiple-choice test. Remember— it's about demonstrating mastery of the concept, not the format of the test.

Designing Accessible Instruction

What tips should I keep in mind when designing accessible instruction?

Learn How They Learn

Your insight into how your students learn will help guide your decisions for using, repurposing, and supplementing the resources within *Into Literature*. You know what your students need better than we do! Use your own style to create instruction, keeping their diversity in mind. Here are some tips that might help.

- **Design instruction that incorporates more than one method of learning.** *Multiple means* is one of the foundational principles of UDL. If you teach aloud, also sketch or project pictures. If you teach with visuals, also provide reading.

- **Consider layout and presentation.** Font choices that work best for students with dyslexia (like Antique Olive), color choices that work best for students with color blindness (high contrast), and whitespace choices that work well for the visually impaired (generous) also work for students who need no accommodations. So why not start with these choices? Also consider presentation. Will you display the lesson on a whiteboard? If so, make sure the marker is thick enough to read from the back of the classroom.

- **Pair images and descriptions.** If you include images in any handouts or slides you develop, provide a description of those images to help visually impaired students understand their meaning.

- **Create captions.** Make sure any instructional videos you produce have captions. Sometimes audio descriptions or more descriptive transcripts are required.

- **Get descriptive.** If you post links or assignments to Ed or to a learning-management system, make sure they have meaningful titles that will make sense to students using screen readers or other assistive technology.

- **Check yourself.** Many popular tools, such as those created by Microsoft and Google®, are inherently accessible and have accessibility-checker features built into the software. Use them!

- **Think through alternatives.** Ask yourself: Will my students require an alternate means of demonstrating knowledge or completing the assignment? Adapt as necessary.

Remember that all of us have abilities—and limits to those abilities. Some limitations are permanent, and others are temporary. Thinking about people with permanent disabilities will result in instruction that benefits people universally.

Professional Learning

134   Surviving Your First Year
       in the Classroom

140   Growing Your Craft
       with **HMH Literacy Solutions**™

142   Growing Your Craft
       with **Teacher's Corner**

Surviving Your First Year in the Classroom

Getting Started

What should I do before students arrive?

Gather Resources

Take time to learn what resources are available to you. You may have more than what is apparent when you walk in your room.

- Take stock of the Student Edition. *Into Literature* is designed for students to have their own consumable print edition and/or digital edition each year. Is that the case at your school? If not, find out how other teachers manage.

- Familiarize yourself with the Teacher's Edition. Far from simply providing answers, this robust tool will help you plan and customize units and lessons; differentiate your teaching to accommodate students who struggle, advanced learners, and English learners; and pull in other resources.

- Make sure you have the credentials for Ed: Your Friend in Learning, the HMH digital platform. Think about how your students will access the platform. The Information Technology team in your school or district can get your students rostered.

- Check out the **Teacher's Corner** on Ed. It includes videos and tutorials that will help you get started with *Into Literature*, improve your craft, and address common teaching challenges.

- Talk to the school librarian and your department head about what novels and research materials are available, and how you can gain access to them.

- Remember that other teachers are your greatest resource. Don't be afraid to ask the veterans in your school for help.

Make Some Plans and Organize Your Room

Figure out which elements of the curriculum are set by your administration and which are up to you. Even if you are working from a mandated list of texts and skills, you will want to have some activities on hand that can keep your students engaged while reinforcing concepts. Ask veteran teachers where they look for ideas.

Make the classroom yours. You don't have to go overboard and fill every space. You'll want room to show students' work as they complete it, and to display anchor charts and reminders that you work on together. But you can add visual interest by showcasing the covers from popular novels, promote positive values by including literary or motivational quotations, and help students get to know you by representing your own interests.

Getting Started

What should I do my first week?

Tips & Tricks!

Follow up the essay with an interest inventory. Write a variety of genres on a flip chart or on pieces of paper taped around the room, and have students write their name next to genres they like.

Get to Know Your Class

Get to know your students through a combination of fun games, an introduction to academics, and assessment.

- Ask students to **organize themselves in groups or lines** according to prompts you call out. You can use variations on this game throughout the year to get students moving and have them take a position on topics introduced in class.

- Read **"Becoming a Better Reader"** on page FM22 and use it as a jumping-off point for a discussion about what students like to read.

- Administer the **HMH Growth Measure**, an adaptive student assessment that measures reading skills and progress, so that you know where your students are starting from and can monitor their growth over the course of the year.

Sample Prompts

Tell students to organize themselves

- in an alphabetical line by first name

- in an alphabetical line by last name

- into groups according to who prefers graphic novels and who prefers prose

- into groups according to who prefers science fiction and who prefers realistic fiction

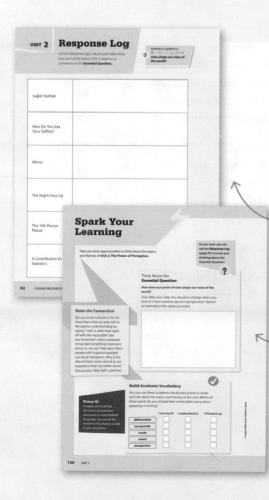

Establish Routines and Set Expectations

You may feel nervous your first few weeks in the classroom, but it's important to project authority and confidence. Fake it until you make it, and know that you won't be the first new teacher to use this trusted strategy.

- Introduce key expectations and routines to your class. Will you have students do a Bell Ringer activity each day? Complete a **Response Log** about the unit's Essential Question at the end of each selection? Tell students what you expect from them, and what they can expect from you.

- Explain grading and preview major milestones. If there's a big project or a well-known unit that students will be working toward, create excitement around it.

- Begin the first unit. Use the **Spark Your Learning** activities in the Student Edition to continue to get to know your students and help them to know each other.

- Assign the first selection. Choose something high-interest that is likely to appeal to a large number of students.

How should I organize my students?

Choose a Purposeful Seating Plan

Whether students are grouped at tables or seated at individual desks, a seating map is a powerful tool. Revise it throughout the year in response to your students' behavior, growth, and academic and social needs.

- Group struggling readers with advanced readers. Encourage higher performers to offer assistance and feedback to students who are having more of a struggle.

- Establish routines for how individuals or groups should move around the room or function independently. Discuss expectations first and model the behavior you wish to see.

- Seat students with behavioral needs closest to wherever you are the most stationary. Proximity is a great way to redirect misbehavior without disrupting the lesson or drawing attention to the student.

- Create a clear and wide path by which you can circulate the room with ease. If you know you spend time conferring with specific students, seat them in areas where your back won't be turned to the rest of the class when you talk to them.

Tips & Tricks!

For certain projects or units, you may want to allow students to choose their own seats. Use this as a motivator for good classroom behavior.

Flexible Grouping Options

Look for other grouping suggestions and independent learning opportunities in each selection's wrap.

Whole Group
Four Corners
- After reading, label the room with these topics: *Juliet; Romeo; Their Parents; Shakespeare's Message*.
- Invite equal numbers of students to go to each area. Within each area, have students form groups of three.
- Prompt students to discuss each author's perspective on that topic. Allow 2–3 minutes for discussion. Then, have students choose a new area and discuss. Repeat until students have visited each area.

Small Group
Say Something
- Before reading, have students form small groups to preview the texts.
- State the title of the first selection: "More than Reckless Teenagers." Signal for students to take turns saying one comment or posing a question about the title.
- Invite students to add on to someone's comment or respond to a question.
- Repeat with the title of the second selection: "Romeo Is a Dirtbag."

Independent Learning
Evaluate the Claims Have students [...] argument evaluating how well the [...] Suggest they evaluate the argument [...] the end-of-unit writing task. Have st[...] with someone who evaluated the s[...]

What activities can I use for grouping or independent learning?

Small Group

Say Something

- Before reading, have students form small groups to preview the texts.

- State the title of the first selection: "More than Reckless Teenagers." Signal for students to take turns saying one comment or posing a question about the title.

- Invite students to add on to someone's comment or respond to a question.

- Repeat with the title of the second selection: "Romeo Is a Dirtbag." Continue as time allows, posing questions or topics that activate students' prior knowledge, set a purpose for reading, and prepare them for analyzing.

Use Flexible Grouping Strategies

Students shouldn't only work in groups with those they're seated with. Variety will help keep them engaged. The **Lesson Planning Guides** and notes in the Teacher's Edition suggest activities designed for whole-class, independent, and small-group learning, including partner activities. Try different strategies for creating groups.

- Group students who struggle with the same skill so that they can receive remediation together.

- Ask students to count off by six and move to work with others who have the same number they do for that day.

- Have students group themselves by birthdays. Those born in January and February work together, those born in March and April work together, and so on.

Ed

Tips & Tricks!

Use the group function on Ed to organize students into groups according to their mastery of certain skills.

Managing Your Class

Set Expectations, Model, and Reflect

Dealing with behavior and classroom management might be a challenge at first, but you've got this. Allow yourself to dial back the amount of material you cover as you figure out management strategies that work in your classroom.

● Make sure you're familiar with any school-wide expectations or behavior programs. Reinforce these with the messaging in your class.

● Keep an eye on students. Face them as much as possible. If a student is being disruptive, try focusing attention on that person with a glance, or by asking a question about the lesson. Often you'll be able to redirect behavior without calling that student out.

● Encourage students by consistently recognizing model behavior. Constantly calling attention to negative behavior can reinforce and increase it. Consider the examples shown on the sticky notes.

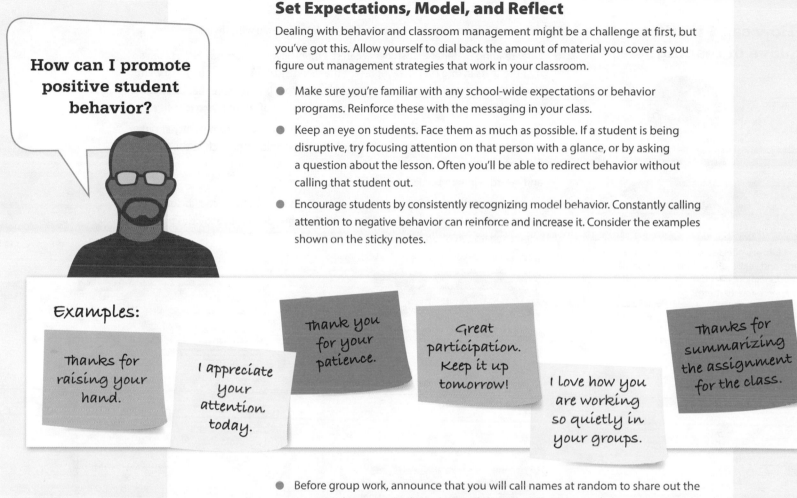

How can I promote positive student behavior?

Examples:

Thanks for raising your hand.

I appreciate your attention today.

Thank you for your patience.

Great participation. Keep it up tomorrow!

I love how you are working so quietly in your groups.

Thanks for summarizing the assignment for the class.

● Before group work, announce that you will call names at random to share out the group's take-aways. Each student in the group will earn a grade based on that one student's response. This ensures all students are invested in the discussion.

● Be mindful that research has shown we all carry unconscious biases, including racial bias. Question your own assumptions and behavior, and reflect on whether you treat different students differently for the same misbehavior. Be ready to adjust your teaching practice as you learn more about your students and yourself.

How can I instill a love of reading?

Tips & Tricks!

The **Text Library** offers selections in a wide range of genres and Lexile® levels. Find opportunities to let students explore the offerings in the Lexile® ranges appropriate to them.

Offer Variety and Choice

Give students opportunities to connect their reading material with their lives.

● Offer reading material that students can see themselves in. Care has been taken so that the texts in *Into Literature* represent the diversity of the world, but you'll want to go beyond that. The website *We Need Diverse Books* is a resource that can help you find titles and authors that appeal to a wide range of cultures and identities.

● Surround students with good books. Work with your school or community librarian as you build your own classroom library. Refer to organizations such as the YALAB (a division of the American Library Association) to keep abreast of new, popular, and award-winning books for young adults.

● Encourage students to make personal connections to what they read, including connections to movies and pop culture. The **Engage Your Brain** activities that open each lesson often offer opportunities to do this.

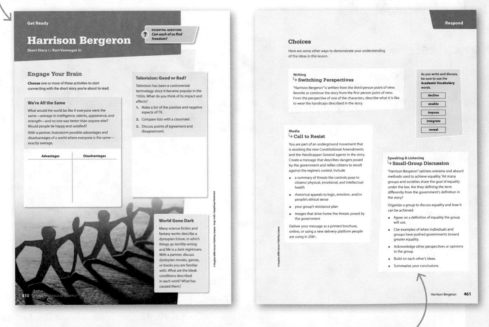

● Allow students to respond to their reading in a variety of ways. Not everything has to be assessed with a quiz or an academic writing assignment. The **Choices** activities at the end of each lesson offer chances for students to respond creatively to assigned reading. For independent reading, you can have students show their understanding through a conversation with you, a video summary, or a poster that shows key literary elements.

● Model your own reading life. If you communicate with students by email, include the title of the book you're reading as part of your signature. Read chunks of text aloud to demonstrate how stories can come alive.

Avoiding Burnout

How do I spend less time grading?

Don't Try to Do It All

Grading, especially the grading of writing, can be an English language arts teacher's biggest time commitment. But there are ways to make it more manageable.

- You do not have to personally grade every assignment. Consider informally monitoring students' progress on lower-stakes assignments.

- If you administer **Selection** and **Unit Tests** online, the platform will do the majority of the work for you. You do need to grade open-response items, but you have the ability to remove them from the test before assigning it.

- During writing time, circulate around the room, pausing to offer explicit feedback to students you know are struggling. This will save you time later.

- Use the **Revision Guide** that accompanies each writing task to model how to evaluate an example of student writing. Then allow students to use the same guide to evaluate each other's drafts.

- Use **Writable** tools. Functions like **Turn It In, Revision Aid**, and anonymous peer reviews can end up saving you time. See "Building Better Writers" in this guide for more details.

Keep Calm and Carry On

The first year in the classroom can definitely be challenging. You have to familiarize yourself with the material, prepare for every lesson, and learn how to meet the requirements of your administration. And that's before the students walk into the classroom! At times, you may feel like you're not getting through to the young learners seated before you. But, more often than not, you probably are, even if they don't show it right away. And if things don't go well today, there's always tomorrow, or next week.

Remember that teaching is a practice that you will refine over time. You don't have to do everything perfectly. It's okay to make mistakes. Seek out the company of other teachers. Learn from them, laugh with them, and take all the help that they'll give you. Soon you'll be in a position to help guide someone else on how to survive and thrive in this meaningful and interesting career.

What if I'm not good at this?

Growing Your Craft with HMH Literacy Solutions™

☺**Ed**

Engaging in Professional Learning

What's the best way to get started using *Into Literature*?

Take the Getting Started Training

Service Training is an important part of using *Into Literature*, and it's designed to be on-going and flexible enough to meet your needs without overwhelming you. The **Getting Started** professional learning session is your first step. It's focused on preparing you for the first few weeks of school.

- Watch classroom videos to see master teachers in action.
- Read articles and get tips from fellow *Into Literature* teachers and other program experts.
- Connect with HMH coaches and thought leaders via live events.

Getting Started Checklist

☑ Visit and bookmark Ed

☑ Take the Getting Started training

☑ Determine the technology needs for your classroom and consider the following questions:
  - Will your students primarily use the print or online version of the Student Edition? Will they use different versions for whole-class instruction and small collaborative groups?
  - When and how will students access the digital Reading, Writing, Grammar, Vocabulary, and Speaking and Listening Resources?
  - Will students access eBooks during independent reading?

☑ As you plan your first unit of instruction, consider teaching one selection according to our recommendations, to get to know all the available resources and features.

How can I make sure I'm getting the most out of *Into Literature*?

Follow up with HMH Literacy Solutions™

As you use the program, questions will arise. **HMH Literacy Solutions™** provides Follow-Up opportunities throughout the year. These shorter sessions allow you to stay engaged and build your expertise in a manageable way. Your school or district can choose from a variety of follow-up topics, including:

- Maximize Learning with Online Resources
- Plan Instruction to Meet Students' Needs
- Make Literacy Accessible for All with Differentiation
- Support English Learners in Reading, Writing, Speaking, and Listening
- Deepen Text Analysis with Notice & Note Close Reading Strategies
- Cultivate Student Voice and Ownership through the Writing Process
- Use **Writable** to Strengthen Writing through Practice, Feedback, and Revision

Tips & Tricks! ☺**Ed**

Visit **Teacher's Corner** on Ed and select **Program Support** to dig deeper into specific areas of *Into Literature*. You will find videos, articles, classroom videos, and more.

Ⴝritable

Participating in Blended Coaching

> **How can I grow as a teacher and improve student outcomes?**

Get Some Coaching

HMH Literacy Solutions™ offers personalized instructional coaching services in districts that have chosen to participate. Coaches use the **Literacy Solutions Instructional Practices Inventory** to focus on both *Into Literature* implementation and evidence-based instructional practices and strategies that increase student outcomes.

To make it easy for you and your HMH coach to stay connected, share resources, upload and reflect on classroom videos, and make continuing progress on learning goals, you will have access to the **HMH Coaching Studio** platform.

Coaching Studio

Coaching Studio is the platform where you'll continue your progress and stay connected with your HMH coach and your colleagues.

HMH Into Literature Blended Coaching Services provide:

- model lessons that illustrate instructional techniques
- support for implementing effective teaching practices
- differentiation strategies to meet the needs of all students
- focus on developing and deepening content knowledge
- analysis of student work samples to assess learning and determine instructional next steps
- facilitation of professional learning communities, cadres, and collaborative learning

Growing Your Craft with Teacher's Corner

What is Teacher's Corner?

A One-Click Solution for Professional Learning

We know that for some things, just-in-time help can be more effective than periodic in-person trainings. **Teacher's Corner** is a section on the learning platform Ed where you can get tips for using *Into Literature*, help with lesson planning, and ideas for improving your instructional practice exactly when you need them. With Teacher's Corner, you have access to on-demand professional learning and teaching support via Ed anytime, anywhere.

- Watch classroom videos to see master teachers in action.
- Read articles and get tips from fellow *Into Literature* teachers and other program experts.
- Connect with HMH coaches and thought leaders via live events.

Explore Recommendations Based on What You Need Now

Choose from a library of bite-size, curated professional learning resources that were designed to be immediately applicable. Some of these can be read or viewed in the time it takes to drink a cup of coffee. Others are longer, but still short enough to fit into your day. The resources come in a variety of media types and are organized into four areas.

How can I get the right help at the right time?

- **Getting Started** offers introductions to *Into Literature* and help with back-to-school planning.
- **Program Support** helps you troubleshoot and get the most out of *Into Literature* as you deepen your teaching.
- **Teacher's Breakroom** gives information about general best practices and lesson ideas, and provides inspiration for teachers across grades and disciplines.
- **Live Events** allows you to register for sessions that are relevant to your needs.

5 Tips for Pacing and Prioritizing Instruction with Into Literature

I once heard someone say: "The minute someone develops a pacing guide, it's out of date." Every school has different state and district mandated instructional days, literacy block/ELA minutes, structures, student numbers, and student needs. The art of teaching is how to use the resources to meet the needs of our students! As a special educator, intervention teacher, ELA and Reading Coordinator, I loved working with teams of teachers to dig into that puzzle. I hope my tips and tricks for pacing and prioritizing will help in your quest to pace and prioritize instruction in your Into Literature classroom. Remember: it's a journey, not an event!

Tip 1: Identify What Drives Your Instruction

When meeting with Into Literature teachers I often ask them a few guiding questions to help inform how to best support them with pacing and prioritizing instruction. As you begin your planning, consider the following:

- What are the student outcomes that you want to see?
- Which activities will be better suited to whole-group, small-group, or independent learning?
- Which activities will be appropriate for which students?

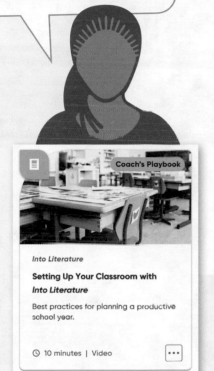

Learning from Peers and Experts

How can I learn from the teachers and coaches who are already using *Into Literature*?

Watch Teachers in Action

Many teachers told HMH that the most useful resources we could provide would be videos showing other teachers successfully using *Into Literature* in their classrooms. This growing bank of videos is available as part of a library of resources that provide authentic models and practical strategies addressing common questions.

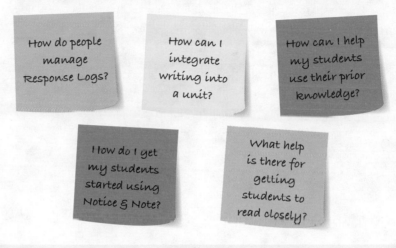

How do people manage Response Logs?

How can I integrate writing into a unit?

How can I help my students use their prior knowledge?

How do I get my students started using Notice & Note?

What help is there for getting students to read closely?

Coach's Playbook

Into Literature

Setting Up Your Classroom with *Into Literature*

Best practices for planning a productive school year.

🕐 10 minutes | Video

How can I connect with other teachers and program experts?

Register for Live Events

Whether you have a question, need implementation advice, or want to keep up with the latest thinking on educational trends, **Live Events** offers you opportunities to connect with HMH coaches and each other. You can register for online sessions that feature everything from groundbreaking new author research to group discussions facilitated by other teachers.

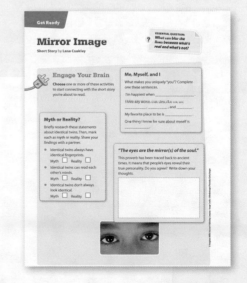

Into Literature
Unit Planning Guides

Get acquainted with each grade level of *HMH Into Literature* by previewing the instructional design of each unit. As you review each **Unit Planning Guide** in Grades 9 and 10, notice

- the unit topic and essential question
- the texts and authors included in the unit, including details about genre, pacing, and Lexile®
- the key skills in reading, writing, vocabulary, and language
- the independent reading options for the unit in the **Reader's Choice** section
- the cumulative tasks in writing and speaking and listening
- digital resources that can support you in teaching each text

146   Grade 9

158   Grade 10

Against All Odds

? **ESSENTIAL QUESTION:** What does it take to survive a crisis?

Analyze & Apply

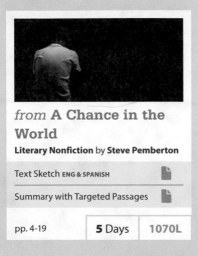

from A Chance in the World
Literary Nonfiction by **Steve Pemberton**

Text Sketch ENG & SPANISH

Summary with Targeted Passages

pp. 4-19 | **5** Days | 1070L

Analyze Literary Nonfiction *   **R**
Analyze Author's Perspective *

Personal Reflection   **W**
Debate
Tribute

Patterns of Word Changes *   **V**

Colons and Semicolons *   **G**

Selection Test   **A**

MENTOR TEXT

Is Survival Selfish?
Argument by **Lane Wallace**

Text Sketch ENG & SPANISH

Summary with Targeted Passages

pp. 20-31 | **4** Days | 1090L

Analyze Arguments *   **R**
Analyze Rhetorical Devices *

Selfish or Smart?   **W**
Group Discussion
Survivor Tales

Synonyms *   **V**

Commas *   **G**

Selection Test   **A**

The Leap
Short Story by **Louis Erdrich**

Text Sketch ENG & SPANISH

Summary with Targeted Passages

pp. 32-47 | **4** Days | 1070L

Analyze Flashback and Tension *   **R**
Make Inferences *

Retell the Story   **W**
Group Discussion
Build a Timeline

Prefixes *   **V**

Relative Clauses *   **G**

Selection Test   **A**

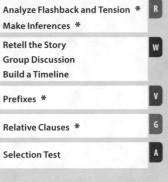

The End and the Beginning
Poem by **Wisława Szymborska**

pp. 48-55 | **4** Days | N/A

Analyze Poetic Language *   **R**
Analyze Poetic Structure * 3

Write a Dialogue   **W**
Podcast
Blog

Selection Test   **A**

SKILLS

R Reading

W Writing/Speaking & Listening/Media

V Vocabulary

G Grammar

A Assessment

* Skills covered on Unit Assessment

RESOURCES

▶ Video

📄 Document

Collaborate & Compare

R Analyze Memoirs *
Analyze Word Choice *

W Create a Flyer
A Life in Art
Multimedia Presentation

V Multiple-Meaning Words *

G Clauses *

A Selection Test

A

from **Night**
Memoir by **Elie Wiesel**

Close Read Screencast ▶

pp. 56–71 | **4** Days | 1070L

B

from **Maus**
Graphic Memoir by **Art Spiegelman**

pp. 72–81 | **4** Days | N/A

R Analyze Graphic Memoirs *
Compare Accounts *

W Draft an Argument
Create a Comic Book
Produce an Oral History

A Selection Test

A **B** pp. 82–83 | **1** Day

Reader's Choice

Find summaries and activities related to Reader's Choice texts on pp. 84–85, and find Reader's Choice texts and tests online.

Adventurers Change. Danger Does Not.
Article by **Alan Cowell**

1160L

from **An Ordinary Man**
Memoir by **Paul Rusesabagina**

980L

Who Understands Me But Me
Poem by
Jimmy Santiago Baca

N/A

Truth at All Costs
Speech by **Marie Colvin**

1060L

from **Deep Survival**
Informational Text by
Laurence Gonzales

950L

Unit Tasks

Against All Odds

pp. 86–97 | **5** Days

W Write an Argument

G Transitions

W Present and Respond to an Argument

W Reflect & Extend
• Author Interview
• Create a Documentary

A Against All Odds Unit Test

Breaking Through Barriers

? **ESSENTIAL QUESTION:**
Are some differences too great to overcome?

Analyze & Apply

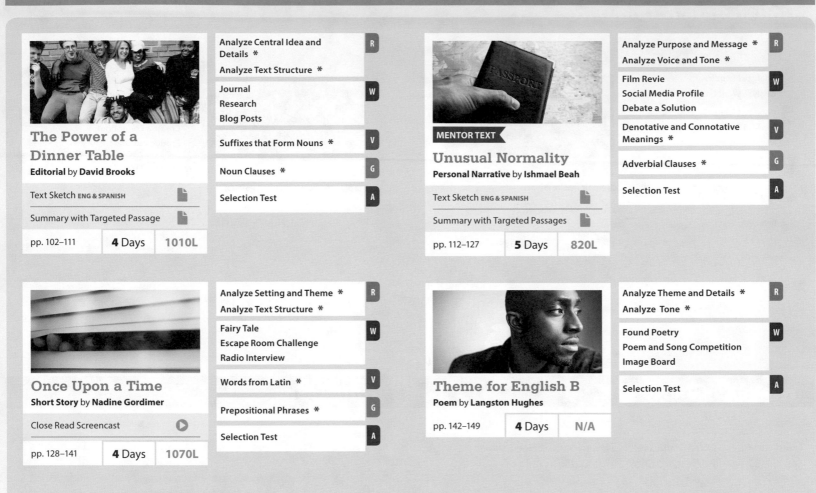

The Power of a Dinner Table
Editorial by David Brooks

Text Sketch ENG & SPANISH

Summary with Targeted Passage

pp. 102–111 | **4** Days | 1010L

R Analyze Central Idea and Details *
Analyze Text Structure *

W Journal
Research
Blog Posts

V Suffixes that Form Nouns *

G Noun Clauses *

A Selection Test

MENTOR TEXT

Unusual Normality
Personal Narrative by Ishmael Beah

Text Sketch ENG & SPANISH

Summary with Targeted Passages

pp. 112–127 | **5** Days | 820L

R Analyze Purpose and Message *
Analyze Voice and Tone *

W Film Revie
Social Media Profile
Debate a Solution

V Denotative and Connotative Meanings *

G Adverbial Clauses *

A Selection Test

Once Upon a Time
Short Story by Nadine Gordimer

Close Read Screencast ▶

pp. 128–141 | **4** Days | 1070L

R Analyze Setting and Theme *
Analyze Text Structure *

W Fairy Tale
Escape Room Challenge
Radio Interview

V Words from Latin *

G Prepositional Phrases *

A Selection Test

Theme for English B
Poem by Langston Hughes

pp. 142–149 | **4** Days | N/A

R Analyze Theme and Details *
Analyze Tone *

W Found Poetry
Poem and Song Competition
Image Board

A Selection Test

Collaborate & Compare

R Analyze Figurative Language*
Analyze Representations in Different Mediums *

W Obituary
Playlist
Brochure

A

The Vietnam Wall
Poem by Alberto Ríos

pp. 150–157 | **2** Days | N/A

B

▶ Views of the Wall
Visual Essay

pp. 158–161 | **3** Days | Media

R Compare Across Genres *

A Selection Test

A **B** pp. 162–163 | **1** Day

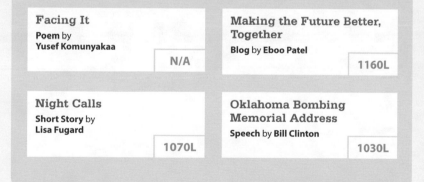

SKILLS

R Reading

W Writing/Speaking & Listening/Media

V Vocabulary

RESOURCES

G Grammar

A Assessment

▶ Video

📄 Document

* Skills covered on Unit Assessment

Collaborate & Compare

R Analyze Author's Purpose and Rhetoric *
Analyze Seminal U.S. Documents *

W Short-Film Screenplay
First-Person Reports
Call to Action

V Multiple-Meaning Words *

G Parallel Structure *

A The Gettysburg Address
Speech by **Abraham Lincoln**
pp. 164–174 | **4** Days | 1140L

B *from* **Saving Lincoln**
Film Clip
pp. 175–179 | **3** Days | Media

R Analyze Media Techniques *
Analyze Media Representations *
Compare Source and Interpretation *

W Letter to Lincoln
Film Analysis
Compare Interpretations

A Selection Test

A B pp. 180–181 | **1** Day

Reader's Choice

Find summaries and activities related to Reader's Choice texts on pp. 182–183, and find Reader's choice texts and tests online.

Facing It
Poem by **Yusef Komunyakaa**
N/A

Making the Future Better, Together
Blog by **Eboo Patel**
1160L

Night Calls
Short Story by **Lisa Fugard**
1070L

Oklahoma Bombing Memorial Address
Speech by **Bill Clinton**
1030L

Unit Tasks

Breaking Through Barriers
pp. 184–193 | **5** Days

W Write a Personal Narrative

G Colons and Semicolons

W Reflect & Extend
· Research and Report
· Create a Photo Essay

A Breaking Through Barriers Unit Test

ESSENTIAL QUESTION:
Who suffers when a crime is committed?

Crime Scenes

Analyze & Apply

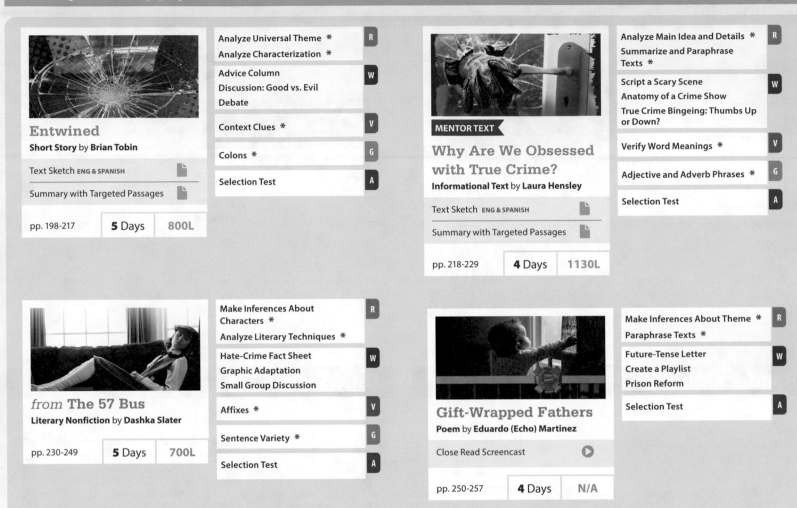

Entwined
Short Story by **Brian Tobin**

Text Sketch ENG & SPANISH

Summary with Targeted Passages

pp. 198-217 | **5** Days | **800L**

Analyze Universal Theme *	R
Analyze Characterization *	
Advice Column	W
Discussion: Good vs. Evil Debate	
Context Clues *	V
Colons *	G
Selection Test	A

MENTOR TEXT

Why Are We Obsessed with True Crime?
Informational Text by **Laura Hensley**

Text Sketch ENG & SPANISH

Summary with Targeted Passages

pp. 218-229 | **4** Days | **1130L**

Analyze Main Idea and Details *	R
Summarize and Paraphrase Texts *	
Script a Scary Scene	W
Anatomy of a Crime Show	
True Crime Bingeing: Thumbs Up or Down?	
Verify Word Meanings *	V
Adjective and Adverb Phrases *	G
Selection Test	A

---

from **The 57 Bus**
Literary Nonfiction by **Dashka Slater**

pp. 230-249 | **5** Days | **700L**

Make Inferences About Characters *	R
Analyze Literary Techniques *	
Hate-Crime Fact Sheet	W
Graphic Adaptation	
Small Group Discussion	
Affixes *	V
Sentence Variety *	G
Selection Test	A

Gift-Wrapped Fathers
Poem by **Eduardo (Echo) Martinez**

Close Read Screencast ▶

pp. 250-257 | **4** Days | **N/A**

Make Inferences About Theme *	R
Paraphrase Texts *	
Future-Tense Letter	W
Create a Playlist	
Prison Reform	
Selection Test	A

© Ed

SKILLS		RESOURCES	
R Reading	**G** Grammar	▶ Video	
W Writing/Speaking & Listening/Media	**A** Assessment	📄 Document	
V Vocabulary	* Skills covered on Unit Assessment		

Collaborate & Compare

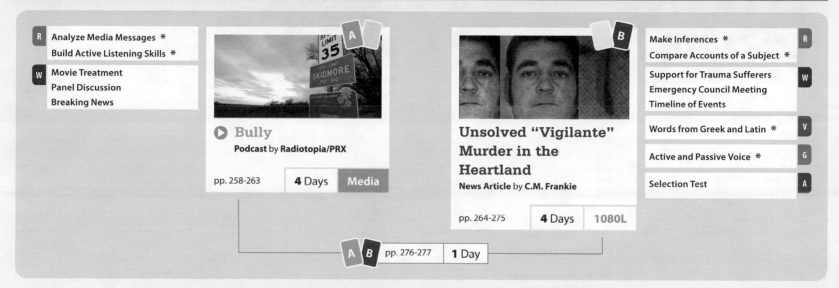

R Analyze Media Messages *
Build Active Listening Skills *

W Movie Treatment
Panel Discussion
Breaking News

A

▶ **Bully**
Podcast by **Radiotopia/PRX**

pp. 258-263   **4 Days**   Media

B

Unsolved "Vigilante" Murder in the Heartland
News Article by **C.M. Frankie**

pp. 264-275   **4 Days**   1080L

R Make Inferences *
Compare Accounts of a Subject *

W Support for Trauma Sufferers
Emergency Council Meeting
Timeline of Events

V Words from Greek and Latin *

G Active and Passive Voice *

A Selection Test

A B pp. 276-277   **1 Day**

Reader's Choice

© Ed

Find summaries and activities related to Reader's Choice texts on pp. 278-279, and find Reader's Choice texts and tests online.

Lamb to the Slaughter
Short Story by **Roald Dahl**
730L

My Afterlife on the Body Farm
Informational Text by **Fawn Fitter**
1320L

The Crime of My Life
Short Story by **Gregg Olsen**
820L

Why Aren't Police Solving More Murders with Genealogy Websites?
Science Writing by **Adam Janos**
1150L

Prometheus Bound
Graphic Short adapted from Aeschylus by **Ellis Rosen**
N/A

Unit Tasks

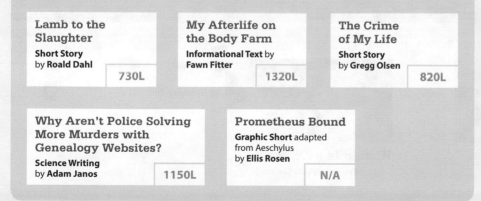

Crime Scenes

pp. 280–291   **5 Days**

W Create an Informative Essay

G Spell Plural Nouns Correctly

W Create a Podcast

W Reflect & Extend
· Create a Sketchnote
· Write an Argument

A Crime Scenes Unit Test

Love and Loss

ESSENTIAL QUESTION:
How can love bring both joy and pain?

Analyze & Apply

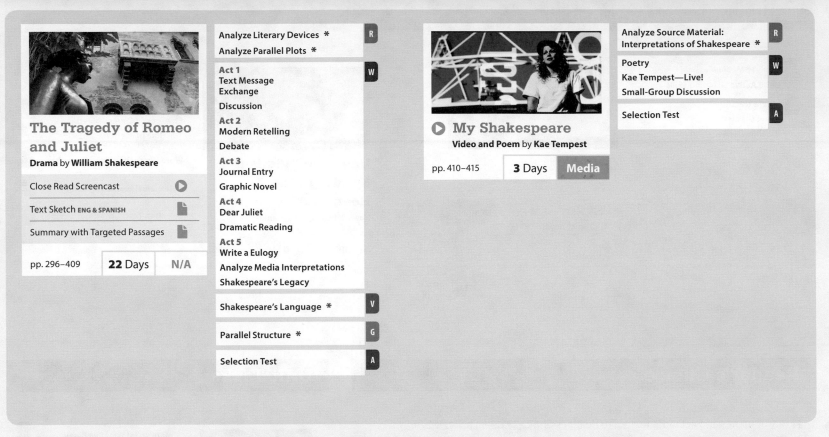

The Tragedy of Romeo and Juliet

Drama by William Shakespeare

Close Read Screencast ▶

Text Sketch ENG & SPANISH 🗎

Summary with Targeted Passages 🗎

pp. 296–409 | **22 Days** | N/A

Analyze Literary Devices * [R]
Analyze Parallel Plots *

Act 1 [W]
Text Message Exchange
Discussion

Act 2
Modern Retelling
Debate

Act 3
Journal Entry
Graphic Novel

Act 4
Dear Juliet
Dramatic Reading

Act 5
Write a Eulogy
Analyze Media Interpretations
Shakespeare's Legacy

Shakespeare's Language * [V]

Parallel Structure * [G]

Selection Test [A]

▶ My Shakespeare

Video and Poem by Kae Tempest

pp. 410–415 | **3 Days** | Media

Analyze Source Material: Interpretations of Shakespeare * [R]

Poetry [W]
Kae Tempest—Live!
Small-Group Discussion

Selection Test [A]

Collaborate & Compare

Compare Authors' Claims * [R]
Analyze Rhetoric *

Sketchnote [W]
Relationships
Argue the Points

Figurative Language * [V]

Verb Phrases * [G]

[A]

MENTOR TEXT

More than Reckless Teenagers

Literary Analysis by Caitlin Smith

Summary with Targeted Passages 🗎

Text Sketch ENG & SPANISH 🗎

pp. 416–423 | **2 Days** | 1130L

[B]

Romeo Is a Dirtbag

Literary Analysis by Lois Leveen

pp. 424–431 | **3 Days** | 1320L

Compare Arguments * [R]

Selection Test [A]

[A] [B] pp. 432–433 | **1 Day**

© Ed

SKILLS

R	Reading
W	Writing/Speaking & Listening/Media
V	Vocabulary

* Skills covered on Unit Assessment

RESOURCES

| G | Grammar |
| A | Assessment |

| ▶ | Video |
| 📄 | Document |

Collaborate & Compare

© Ed

| R | Analyze Source Material * |
| | Analyze Structure * |

W	Sad Love Story
	Ovid's Metamorphoses
	Reader's Theater

A

Pyramus and Thisbe
from **Metamorphoses**
Myth by **Ovid**

Online | N/A

B

from **Romeo and Juliet**
Drama by **William Shakespeare**

Online | N/A

| Compare Source and Adaptation * | R |
| Selection Test | A |

Reader's Choice

© Ed

Find summaries and activities related to Reader's Choice texts on pp. 434–435, and find Reader's choice texts and tests online.

| **Sorry for Your Loss** Short Story by **Lisa Rubenson** | 500L |

| **The Price of Freedom** Personal Essay by **Noreen Riols** | 760L |

| **The Bass, the River, and Sheila Mant** Short Story by **W.D. Wetherell** | 1060L |

| **Sonnet 71** Sonnet by **Pablo Neruda** | N/A |

| *from* **Why Love Literally Hurts** Science Writing by **Eric Jaffe** | 1260L |

Unit Tasks

Love and Loss
pp. 436–445 | **5** Days

Write a Literary Analysis	W
Check Capitalization	G
Reflect & Extend • Create a Comic Strip • Write a Short Story	W
Love and Loss Unit Test	A

Freedom at All Costs

Analyze & Apply

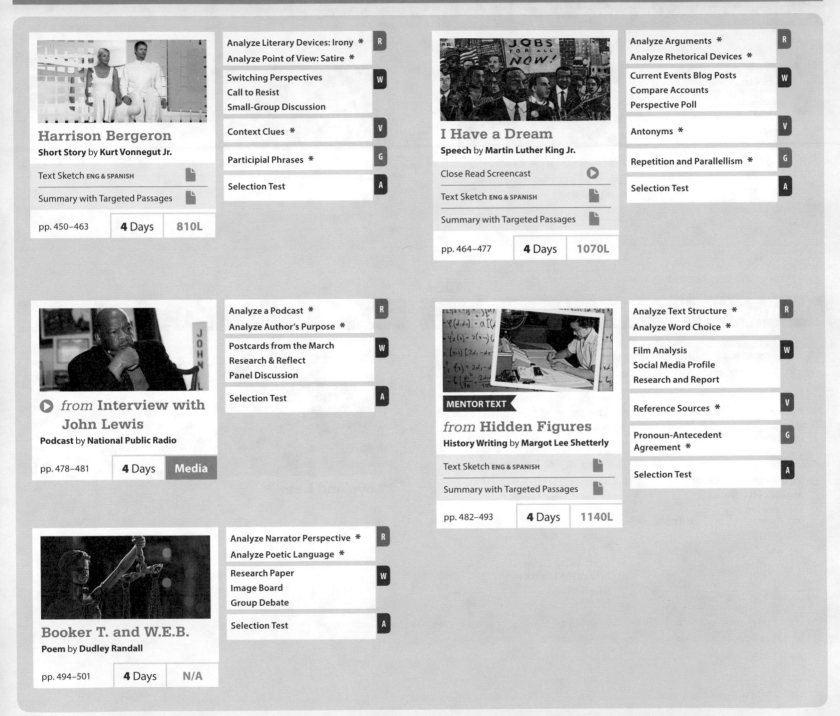

Harrison Bergeron
Short Story by **Kurt Vonnegut Jr.**

Text Sketch ENG & SPANISH

Summary with Targeted Passages

pp. 450–463 | **4** Days | 810L

Analyze Literary Devices: Irony *   R
Analyze Point of View: Satire *

Switching Perspectives   W
Call to Resist
Small-Group Discussion

Context Clues *   V

Participial Phrases *   G

Selection Test   A

I Have a Dream
Speech by **Martin Luther King Jr.**

Close Read Screencast

Text Sketch ENG & SPANISH

Summary with Targeted Passages

pp. 464–477 | **4** Days | 1070L

Analyze Arguments *   R
Analyze Rhetorical Devices *

Current Events Blog Posts   W
Compare Accounts
Perspective Poll

Antonyms *   V

Repetition and Parallellism *   G

Selection Test   A

---

from Interview with John Lewis
Podcast by **National Public Radio**

pp. 478–481 | **4** Days | Media

Analyze a Podcast *   R
Analyze Author's Purpose *

Postcards from the March   W
Research & Reflect
Panel Discussion

Selection Test   A

MENTOR TEXT

from Hidden Figures
History Writing by **Margot Lee Shetterly**

Text Sketch ENG & SPANISH

Summary with Targeted Passages

pp. 482–493 | **4** Days | 1140L

Analyze Text Structure *   R
Analyze Word Choice *

Film Analysis   W
Social Media Profile
Research and Report

Reference Sources *   V

Pronoun-Antecedent Agreement *   G

Selection Test   A

Booker T. and W.E.B.
Poem by **Dudley Randall**

pp. 494–501 | **4** Days | N/A

Analyze Narrator Perspective *   R
Analyze Poetic Language *

Research Paper   W
Image Board
Group Debate

Selection Test   A

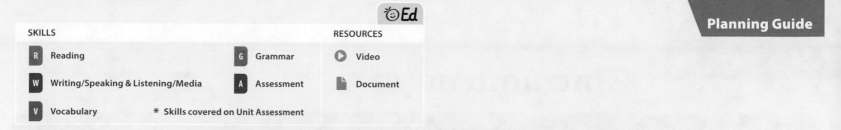
SKILLS

R Reading

W Writing/Speaking & Listening/Media

V Vocabulary

RESOURCES

G Grammar

A Assessment

▶ Video

📄 Document

* Skills covered on Unit Assessment

Collaborate & Compare

R Analyze Rhetorical Devices *
Analyze Setting and Purpose *

W Journal Entry
Timeline
Podcast

V Denotative and Connotative
Meanings *

G Verb Tense *

A

from **Reading Lolita in Tehran**
Memoir by **Azar Nafisi**

pp. 502–513   **4** Days   **1110L**

B

from **Persepolis 2: The Story of a Return**
Graphic Memoir by **Marjane Satrapi**

pp. 514–519   **4** Days   **N/A**

R Determine Author's
Point of View *
Analyze Accounts in
Different Mediums *
Compare Treatments of a Topic *

W Analysis
Graphic Short
Small-Group Debate

A Selection Test

A B pp. 520–521   **1** Day

Reader's Choice

Find summaries and activities related to Reader's Choice texts on pp. 522–523, and find Reader's Choice texts and tests online.

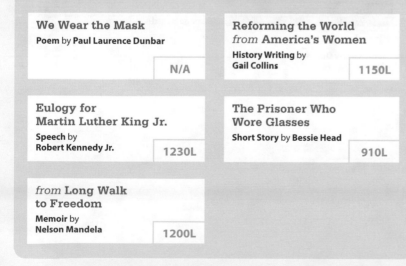

We Wear the Mask
Poem by **Paul Laurence Dunbar**

N/A

Eulogy for Martin Luther King Jr.
Speech by **Robert Kennedy Jr.**

1230L

from **Long Walk to Freedom**
Memoir by **Nelson Mandela**

1200L

Reforming the World
from **America's Women**
History Writing by **Gail Collins**

1150L

The Prisoner Who Wore Glasses
Short Story by **Bessie Head**

910L

Unit Tasks

Freedom at All Costs

pp. 524–533   **5** Days

W Write a Research Report

G Pronoun-Antecedent Agreement

W Reflect & Extend
· Create a Protest Song
· Write a Poem

A Freedom at All Costs Unit Test

Epic Journeys

ESSENTIAL QUESTION:
What drives us to take on a challenge?

Analyze & Apply

from **The Odyssey**

Epic Poem by **Homer**, translated by **Robert Fitzgerald**

Close Read Screencast ▶

Text Sketch ENG & SPANISH 📄

Summary with Targeted Passages 📄

pp. 538–565 | **5 Days** | N/A

Analyze Character: Epic Hero *	**R**
Analyze Epic Poetry *	
Switching Perspectives	**W**
Graphic Adaptation	
Research and Record	
Words from Latin *	**V**
Absolute Phrases *	**G**
Selection Test	**A**

MENTOR TEXT

Archaeology's Tech Revolution

Informational Text by **Jeremy Hsu**

Text Sketch ENG & SPANISH 📄

Summary with Targeted Passages 📄

pp. 566–577 | **4 Days** | 1330L

Make Predictions *	**R**
Determine Central Idea *	
Research and Report	**W**
Virtual Tour	
Small-Group Discussion	
Use References *	**V**
Use Appositives Effectively *	**G**
Selection Test	**A**

Collaborate & Compare

R	Analyze Ideas and Events *
	Evaluate Graphic Features *
W	Blog Posts
	Community Tour
	Maze Challenge
V	Word Roots *
G	Sentence Variety *

A

from **The Cruelest Journey: 600 Miles to Timbuktu**

Travel Writing by **Kira Salak**

pp. 578–593 | **4 Days** | 990L

B

The Journey

Poem by **Mary Oliver**

pp. 594–601 | **4 Days** | N/A

Interpret Figurative Language *	**R**
Make Connections *	
Compare Messages Across Genres *	
Music Connection	**W**
Image Board	
Journal Entry	
Selection Test	**A**

A B pp. 602–603 | **1 Day**

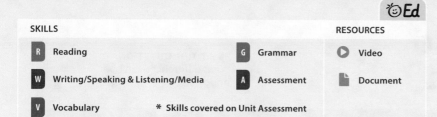

SKILLS

R Reading

W Writing/Speaking & Listening/Media

V Vocabulary

G Grammar

A Assessment

* Skills covered on Unit Assessment

RESOURCES

▶ Video

📄 Document

Reader's Choice

Find summaries and activities related to Reader's Choice texts on pp. 604–605, and find Reader's Choice texts and tests online.

from The Odyssey
Epic Poem by **Homer**
N/A

from The Odyssey: A Dramatic Retelling of Homer's Epic
Drama by **Simon Armitage**
N/A

Siren Song
Poem by **Margaret Atwood**
N/A

Ilse, Who Saw Clearly
Short Story by **E. Lily Yu**
830L

The Real Reasons We Explore Space
Argument by **Michael Griffin**
1140L

Unit Tasks

Epic Journeys

pp. 606–617   **5** Days

Write an Expository Essay **W**

Spell Commonly Confused Words Correctly **G**

Participate in a Collaborative Discussion **W**

Reflect & Extend **W**
• Create a Movie Trailer
• Write a Play

Epic Journeys Unit Test **A**

Conflict and Connection

Analyze & Apply

The Book of the Dead
Short Story by Edwidge Dantica

Text Sketch ENG & SPANISH

Summary with Targeted Passages

| pp. 4-23 | **5** Days | **920L** |

Analyze Development of Theme * | **R**
Understand Cultural and Historical Context *

Write a Letter | **W**
Visual Art
Haitian History

Oxymoron * | **V**

Noun Phrases and Verb Phrases * | **G**

Selection Test | **A**

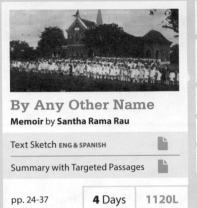

By Any Other Name
Memoir by Santha Rama Rau

Text Sketch ENG & SPANISH

Summary with Targeted Passages

| pp. 24-37 | **4** Days | **1120L** |

Analyze Historical Context * | **R**
Analyze Author's Purpose *

Write an Argument | **W**
Group Discussion
Name Changes in History

Words from Other Languages in English * | **V**

Appropriate Verb Tense * | **G**

Selection Test | **A**

Without Title
Poem by Diane Glancy

| pp. 38-45 | **4** Days | **N/A** |

Analyze Setting * | **R**
Make Inferences About Theme *

Write a Poem | **W**
Cultural Change
Contrast Collage

Selection Test | **A**

What, of This Goldfish, Would You Wish?
Short Story by Etgar Kere

Close Read Screencast ▶

Text Sketch ENG & SPANISH

Summary with Targeted Passages

| pp. 46-59 | **4** Days | **1110L** |

Analyze Character Motivations * | **R**
Analyze Cultural Background *

Media Montage | **W**
Write a Fable
Compare Archetypes

Context Clues * | **V**

Tone * | **G**

Selection Test | **A**

SKILLS

R Reading

W Writing/Speaking & Listening/Media

V Vocabulary

G Grammar

A Assessment

* Skills covered on Unit Assessment

RESOURCES

▶ Video

📄 Document

Collaborate & Compare

R Analyze Seminal Documents *
Evaluate Evidence *

W Write a Comparison
Discuss Rights
Current Events

V Words from Latin *

G Noun Clauses *

A **B**

from **Texas v. Johnson**

Court Opinions by William J. Brennan and William Rehnquist

Close Read Screencast ▶

Adaptation with Targeted Passages 📄

| pp. 60-73 | **5** Days | 1110L/1300L |

C

MENTOR TEXT

American Flag Stands for Tolerance

Editorial by Ronald J. Alle

Close Read Screencast ▶

Text Sketch ENG & SPANISH 📄

Summary with Targeted Passages 📄

| pp. 74-83 | **4** Days | 1130L |

R Evaluate an Argument *
Analyze Rhetoric *
Compare Arguments *

W Letter to the Editor
Debate the Issue
Negotiate Conflict

V Connotations *

G Diction and Tone *

A Selection Test

A **B** **C** | pp. 84-85 | **1** Day |

Reader's Choice

Find summaries and activities related to Reader's Choice texts on pp. 86–87, and find Reader's Choice texts and tests online.

| *from* **The Pleasure of Reading** **Memoir** by **Kamila Shamsie** | 1270L |

| **Magic Island** **Poem** by **Cathy Song** | N/A |

| **America: The Multinational Society** **Argument** by **Ishmael Reed** | 1440L |

| **The Wife's Story** **Short Story** by **Ursula K. Le Guin** | 780L |

| **The Lottery** **Short Story** by **Shirley Jackson** | 1030L |

Unit Tasks

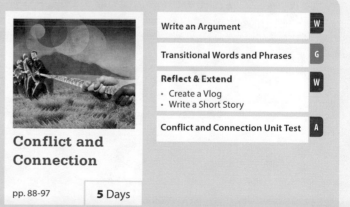

W Write an Argument

G Transitional Words and Phrases

W Reflect & Extend
• Create a Vlog
• Write a Short Story

A Conflict and Connection Unit Test

Conflict and Connection

| pp. 88-97 | **5** Days |

The Power of Perception

ESSENTIAL QUESTION:
How does our point of view shape our view of the world?

Analyze & Apply

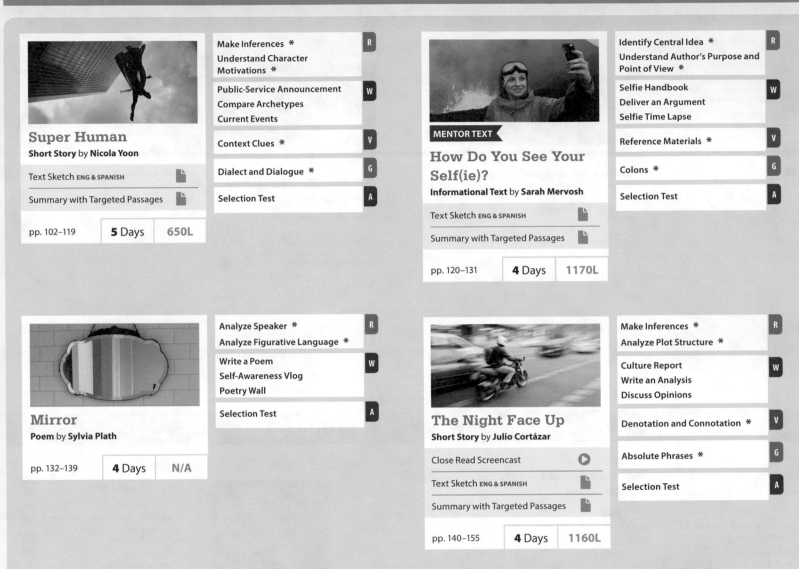

Super Human
Short Story by Nicola Yoon

Text Sketch ENG & SPANISH

Summary with Targeted Passages

pp. 102–119 | **5 Days** | **650L**

Make Inferences *
Understand Character Motivations * **R**

Public-Service Announcement
Compare Archetypes
Current Events **W**

Context Clues * **V**

Dialect and Dialogue * **G**

Selection Test **A**

MENTOR TEXT

How Do You See Your Self(ie)?
Informational Text by Sarah Mervosh

Text Sketch ENG & SPANISH

Summary with Targeted Passages

pp. 120–131 | **4 Days** | **1170L**

Identify Central Idea *
Understand Author's Purpose and Point of View * **R**

Selfie Handbook
Deliver an Argument
Selfie Time Lapse **W**

Reference Materials * **V**

Colons * **G**

Selection Test **A**

Mirror
Poem by Sylvia Plath

pp. 132–139 | **4 Days** | **N/A**

Analyze Speaker *
Analyze Figurative Language * **R**

Write a Poem
Self-Awareness Vlog
Poetry Wall **W**

Selection Test **A**

The Night Face Up
Short Story by Julio Cortázar

Close Read Screencast ▶

Text Sketch ENG & SPANISH

Summary with Targeted Passages

pp. 140–155 | **4 Days** | **1160L**

Make Inferences *
Analyze Plot Structure * **R**

Culture Report
Write an Analysis
Discuss Opinions **W**

Denotation and Connotation * **V**

Absolute Phrases * **G**

Selection Test **A**

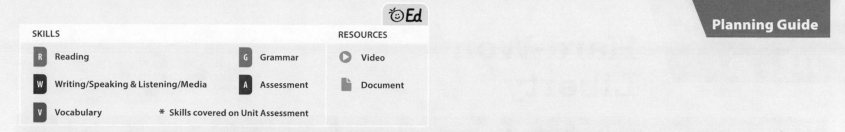

© Houghton Mifflin Harcourt Publishing Company • Image Credits: (tl) ©Science Photo Library/NASA/NOAA/Brand X Pictures/Getty Images; (tr) ©Orbon Alija/E+/Getty Images

SKILLS

R Reading

W Writing/Speaking & Listening/Media

V Vocabulary

RESOURCES

G Grammar

A Assessment

▶ Video

Document

* Skills covered on Unit Assessment

Collaborate & Compare

R Interpret Graphics *
Analyze Motives *

W Write an Advice Letter
Conduct a Poll
Create an Infographic

A

The 100-Person Planet
Infographic

pp. 156–161 | **2** Days | Media

A Contribution to Statistics
Poem by **Wisława Szymborska**

pp. 162–169 | **3** Days | N/A

B

Analyze Literary Devices *
Compare Details * **R**

Selection Test **A**

A **B** pp. 170–171 | **1** Day

Reader's Choice

Find summaries and activities related to Reader's Choice texts on pp. 172–173, and find Reader's Choice texts and tests online.

Before I got my eye put out
Poem by **Emily Dickinson**
N/A

What Our Telescopes Couldn't See
Essay by **Pippa Goldschmidt**
1210L

Why Seeing (the Unexpected) Is Often Not Believing
Informational Text by **Alix Spiegel**
1040L

The Handsomest Drowned Man in the World
Short Story by **Gabriel García Márquez**
1570L

The Police Officer Who Saved Her Life
News Article by **Edgar Sandoval**
1000L

Unit Tasks

The Power of Perception

pp. 174–185 | **5** Days

Write an Explanation **W**

Use Parallel Structure **G**

Deliver a Multimedia Presentation **W**

Reflect & Extend **W**
• Create a Perspective Map
• Write a Narrative Poem

The Power of Perception Unit Test **A**

Hard-Won Liberty

ESSENTIAL QUESTION:
How can we escape what oppresses us?

Analyze & Apply

Letter from Birmingham Jail
Argument by **Martin Luther King Jr.**

Text Sketch ENG & SPANISH

Summary with Targeted Passages

Close Read Screencast

pp. 190–215 | **5** Days | **1160L**

Analyze Argument * — R
Analyze Rhetorical Devices *

Seminal Documents — W
Civil Rights Leaders
Current Events

Context Clues * — V

Repetition and Parallelism * — G

Selection Test — A

The American Embassy
Short Story by **Chimamanda Ngozi Adichie**

Text Sketch ENG & SPANISH

pp. 216–235 | **5** Days | **1020L**

Analyze Character Development * — R
Plot Structure: Flashback *

Epilogue — W
Propose a Solution
Research Immigrant Accounts

Verify Word Meanings * — V

Adjectival Phrases * — G

Selection Test — A

The Hawk Can Soar
Memoir by **Randi Davenport**

pp. 236–247 | **4** Days | **790L**

Analyze Diction and Syntax * — R
Analyze Text Structure *

Policy Analysis — W
Persuasive Letter
Group Discussion

Allusions * — V

Purposeful Fragments * — G

Selection Test — A

©**Ed**

from **The Four Freedoms**
Speech by **Franklin D. Roosevelt**

Online | **1220L**

Analyze Central Idea * — R
Analyze Purpose *

Argument — W
Presidential Speeches
History Timeline

Selection Test — A

Collaborate & Compare

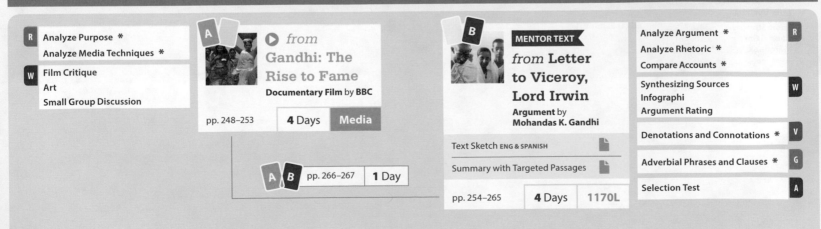

R — Analyze Purpose *
Analyze Media Techniques *

W — Film Critique
Art
Small Group Discussion

A — *from* **Gandhi: The Rise to Fame**
Documentary Film by **BBC**

pp. 248–253 | **4** Days | Media

A B pp. 266–267 | **1** Day

B — **MENTOR TEXT**
from **Letter to Viceroy, Lord Irwin**
Argument by **Mohandas K. Gandhi**

Text Sketch ENG & SPANISH

Summary with Targeted Passages

pp. 254–265 | **4** Days | **1170L**

Analyze Argument * — R
Analyze Rhetoric *
Compare Accounts *

Synthesizing Sources — W
Infographi
Argument Rating

Denotations and Connotations * — V

Adverbial Phrases and Clauses * — G

Selection Test — A

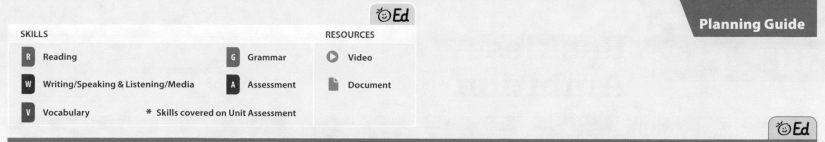

SKILLS

R	Reading
W	Writing/Speaking & Listening/Media
V	Vocabulary

* Skills covered on Unit Assessment

RESOURCES

| G | Grammar |
| A | Assessment |

| ▶ | Video |
| 📄 | Document |

Collaborate & Compare

🙂**Ed**

R	Analyze Elements of Myth *
	Analyze Universal Themes *
W	Myth Adaptation
	Group Discussion
	Problem-Solving Skills

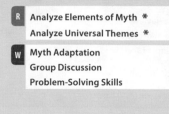
A

from **Popol Vuh**
Myth translated by **Dennis Tedlock**

Online | 640L

B C

The Hero Twins Against the Lords of Death
Graphic Novel by **Dan Jolley** and **David Witt**

Myth-Interpretation
Poem by **Monica Moreno**

Online | N/A

| Compare Source and Adaptations * | R |
| Selection Test | A |

Reader's Choice

🙂**Ed**

Find summaries and activities related to Reader's Choice texts on pp. 268–269, and find Reader's Choice texts and tests online.

from **Speech at the March on Washington**
Speech by **Josephine Baker** | 880L

Elsewhere
Poem by **Derek Walcott** | N/A

Cranes
Short Story by **Hwang Sun-wŏn** | 790L

Cloudy Day
Poem by **Jimmy Santiago Baca** | N/A

Crispus Attucks
History by **Kareem Abdul-Jabbar** | 970L

Unit Tasks

Hard-Won Liberty

pp. 270–281 | **5** Days

Write an Argument	W
Deliver an Argument	
Conventions of Argument	G
Reflect & Extend	W
· Create a Protest Song	
· Write a Biography	
Hard-Won Liberty Unit Test	A

Reckless Ambition

ESSENTIAL QUESTION:
When is ambition dangerous?

Analyze & Apply

The Tragedy of Macbeth

Drama by **William Shakespeare**

Close Read Screencast ▶

Text Sketch ENG & SPANISH 📄

Summary
with Targeted Passages 📄

| pp. 286–375 | **17** Days | N/A |

Analyze Drama * **R**
Analyze Character and Theme *
Analyze Figurative Language *

Act I **W**
Character Contrast
Discuss Plots
Act II
Character Chat
Argue Opinions
Act III
Critical Evaluation
Irony Analysis
Act IV
Job Description
Debate
Act V
Character Evaluation
Group Discussion
Developing Questions

Archaic Language * **V**

Inverted Sentence Structure * **G**

Selection Test **A**

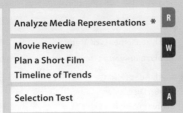

▶ *from* Macbeth
Film by **Rupert Goold**

| pp. 376–379 | **4** Days | Media |

Analyze Media Representations * **R**

Movie Review **W**
Plan a Short Film
Timeline of Trends

Selection Test **A**

SKILLS

R Reading

W Writing/Speaking & Listening/Media

V Vocabulary

RESOURCES

G Grammar

A Assessment

⊙ Ed

▶ Video

📄 Document

* Skills covered on Unit Assessment

Collaborate & Compare

R Analyze Visual Elements *
Analyze Evidence *

W Comparison
Deliver a Pitch
Expert Review

V Word Roots *

G Parentheses *

A

from **Manga Shakespeare: Macbeth**

Graphic Novel by Robert Deas and **Richard Appignanesi**

pp. 380–397 | **2** Days | N/A

B

MENTOR TEXT

Shakespeare and Samurai (and Robot Ninjas?)

Book Review by Caitlin Perry

Text Sketch ENG & SPANISH 📄

Summary
with Targeted Passages 📄

pp. 398–403 | **2** Days | 1480L

Compare Across Genres * **R**

Selection Test **A**

A **B** pp. 404–405 | **1** Day

⊙ Ed

Reader's Choice

Find summaries and activities related to Reader's Choice texts on pp. 406–407, and find Reader's Choice texts and tests online.

from **Holinshed's Chronicles**

History Writing by Raphael Holinshed | 1110L

The Macbeth Murder Mystery

Short Story by James Thurber | 1110L

Julius Caesar, Act III, Scene 2

Drama by William Shakespeare | N/A

Why Read Shakespeare?

Argument by Michael Mack | 1110L

Ozymandias

Poem by Percy Bysshe Shelley | N/A

The Forgotten Story of Orson Welles' All Black 'Macbeth' Production

Informational Text by Kashann Kilson | 1360L

Unit Tasks

Reckless Ambition

pp. 408–417 | **5** Days

Write a Literary Analysis **W**

Check Spelling **G**

Reflect & Extend **W**
· Create a Photo Essay
· Write a Drama

Reckless Ambition Unit Test **A**

Forces of Change

ESSENTIAL QUESTION:
How do changes, large and small, affect us?

Analyze & Apply

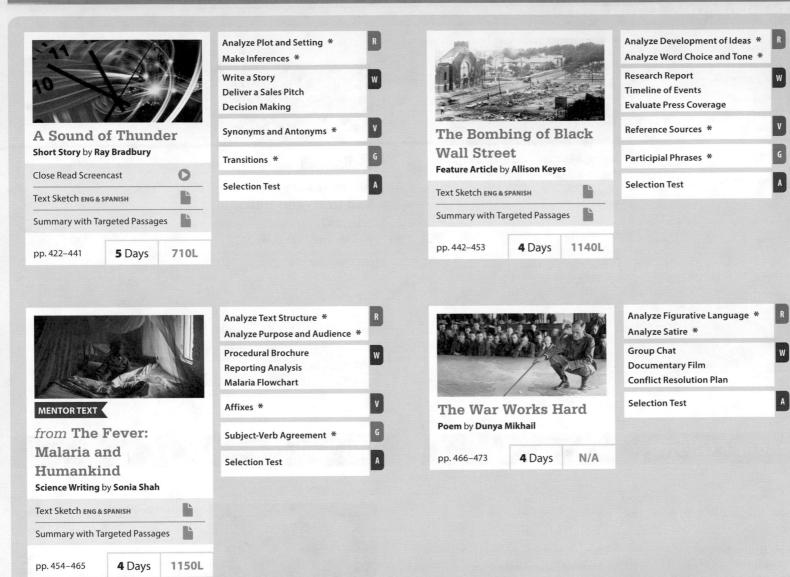

A Sound of Thunder
Short Story by **Ray Bradbury**

Close Read Screencast

Text Sketch ENG & SPANISH

Summary with Targeted Passages

pp. 422–441 | **5** Days | 710L

Analyze Plot and Setting * — R
Make Inferences *

Write a Story — W
Deliver a Sales Pitch
Decision Making

Synonyms and Antonyms * — V

Transitions * — G

Selection Test — A

The Bombing of Black Wall Street
Feature Article by **Allison Keyes**

Text Sketch ENG & SPANISH

Summary with Targeted Passages

pp. 442–453 | **4** Days | 1140L

Analyze Development of Ideas * — R
Analyze Word Choice and Tone *

Research Report — W
Timeline of Events
Evaluate Press Coverage

Reference Sources * — V

Participial Phrases * — G

Selection Test — A

MENTOR TEXT

from **The Fever: Malaria and Humankind**
Science Writing by **Sonia Shah**

Text Sketch ENG & SPANISH

Summary with Targeted Passages

pp. 454–465 | **4** Days | 1150L

Analyze Text Structure * — R
Analyze Purpose and Audience *

Procedural Brochure — W
Reporting Analysis
Malaria Flowchart

Affixes * — V

Subject-Verb Agreement * — G

Selection Test — A

The War Works Hard
Poem by **Dunya Mikhail**

pp. 466–473 | **4** Days | N/A

Analyze Figurative Language * — R
Analyze Satire *

Group Chat — W
Documentary Film
Conflict Resolution Plan

Selection Test — A

SKILLS

R Reading

W Writing/Speaking & Listening/Media

V Vocabulary

RESOURCES

G Grammar

A Assessment

▶ Video

📄 Document

* Skills covered on Unit Assessment

Collaborate & Compare

R Analyze Media Techniques *
Analyze Purpose and Theme *1

W Collaborative Essay
Change Presentation
Reflect on Emotions

▶ *from* Rivers and Tides

Documentary Film by **Thomas Riedelsheimer**

pp. 474–477 | **2 Days** | Media

A

Sonnets to Orpheus, Part Two, XII

Poem by **Rainer Maria Rilke**

pp. 478–481 | **3 Days** | N/A

B

Compare Themes Across Genres * **R**

Compare and Present **W**

Selection Test **A**

A B pp. 482–483 | **1 Day**

Reader's Choice

Find summaries and activities related to Reader's Choice texts on pp. 484–485, and find Reader's Choice texts and tests online.

A Monument to Revolutionary Trans Activists
Informational Article by **Anne Branigin**
1510L

The Norwegian Rat
Short Story by **Naguib Mahfouz**
990L

After the Storm
Memoir by **Orhan Pamuk**
1330L

from **The Unthinkable**
Informational Text by **Amanda Ripley**
800L

Unit Tasks

Forces of Change
pp. 486–495 | **5 Days**

Write a Research Report **W**

Use Transitions and Domain-Specific Language **G**

Reflect & Extend **W**
· Create an Infographic
· Write a Poem

Forces of Change Unit Test **A**

Our Place in Nature

ESSENTIAL QUESTION:
What effect do we have on nature, and how does nature affect us?

Analyze & Apply

The Great Silence
Short Story by Ted Chiang

Close Read Screencast

Text Sketch ENG & SPANISH

Summary with Targeted Passages

pp. 500–511 | **4** Days | **850L**

Analyze Point of View * **R**
Analyze Narrative Structure *

Short Story **W**
Presentation
Communication Strategies

Multiple-Meaning Words * **V**

Parallel Structure * **G**

Selection Test **A**

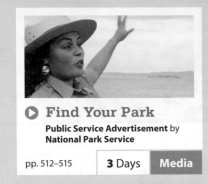

▶ Find Your Park
Public Service Advertisement by National Park Service

pp. 512–515 | **3** Days | Media

Analyze Media Techniques and Purposes * **W**
Letter to the Editor
Advertisement
Problem Solving

Selection Test **A**

MENTOR TEXT

Night Garden
Short Story by Shruti Swamy

Text Sketch ENG & SPANISH

Summary with Targeted Passages

pp. 516–529 | **4** Days | **650L**

Analyze Pacing and Tension * **R**
Analyze Figurative Language *

Literary Analysis **W**
Photo Essay
Group Discussion

Verify Word Meanings * **V**

Relative Clauses * **G**

Selection Test **A**

Can Genetic Engineering Solve the Problem We Created?
Argument by Sarah Zhang

pp. 530–541 | **4** Days | **1260L**

Monitor Comprehension * **R**
Analyze Pro-Con Organization *

Collaborative Blog **W**
Problem-Solution Graphic
Debate

Reference Resources * **V**

Colons, Semicolons, and Dashes * **G**

Selection Test **A**

© Houghton Mifflin Harcourt Publishing Company • Image Credits: (tl) ©K.C. Wilsey/FEMA/Alamy; (tr) Find Your Park: ©National Park Service, D.C.; (bl) ©Aleksandar Kamasi/Shutterstock; (br) ©Carolyn Jenkins/Alamy

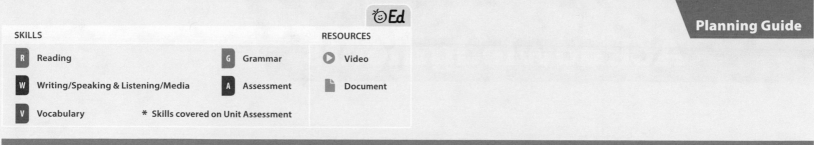
Collaborate & Compare

R Analyze Symbol and Theme *
  Analyze Plot *

W Research Report
  Video Scrapbook
  Advice Podcast

V Figurative Language *

G Complex Sentences *

A **The Seventh Man**
Short Story by **Haruki Murakami**

pp. 542–565   **5** Days   890L

B **Carry**
Poem by **Linda Hogan**

pp. 566–573   **4** Days   N/A

R Analyze Symbol and Theme *
  Analyze Figurative Language *
  Compare Themes *

W Argument
  Photo Analysis
  Discussion

A Selection Test

A B pp. 574–575   **1** Day

Reader's Choice

Find summaries and activities related to Reader's Choice texts on pp. 576–577, and find Reader's Choice texts and tests online.

from **Sand's End**
Informational Text by **Josh Dzieza**

1220L

Even if you live in a city, you can get health benefits from nature
Argument by **Kate Baggaley**   1250L

Starfish
Poem by **Lorna Dee Cervantes**

N/A

Flying Jewels
Essay by **Brian Doyle**

1170L

Wolves
Short Story by **José Luis Zárate**

740L

Unit Tasks

Our Place in Nature

pp. 578–589   **5** Days

W Write a Short Story

G Punctuate Dialogue

W Produce a Podcast

W Reflect & Extend
  · Create a Public Service Advertisement
  · Write an Article

A Our Place in Nature Unit Test

Acknowledgments

Excerpts and cover illustration from *A Chance in the World* by Steve Pemberton. Text copyright © 2012 by Stephen J. Pemberton. Illustration copyright © 2012 by Thomas Nelson. Reprinted by permission of Thomas Nelson. www.thomasnelson.com

Cover illustration from *Life of Pi* by Yann Martel. Illustration copyright © 2003 by Houghton Mifflin Harcourt Publishing Company. Reprinted by permission of Houghton Mifflin Harcourt Publishing Company.

Cover illustration from *The Namesake* by Jhumpa Lahiri. Illustration copyright © 2019 by Houghton Mifflin Harcourt Publishing Company. Reprinted by permission of Houghton Mifflin Harcourt Publishing Company.

Cover illustration from *The Princess Bride* by William Goldman. Illustration copyright © 2007 by Houghton Mifflin Harcourt Publishing Company. Reprinted by permission of Houghton Mifflin Harcourt Publishing Company.

Excerpts from "Thank You, M'am" from *Short Stories* by Langston Hughes. Text copyright © 1996 by Ramona Bass and Arnold Rampersad. Reprinted by permission of Hill and Wang, a division of Farrar, Straus and Giroux and Harold Ober Associates Incorporated. CAUTION: Users are warned that this work is protected under copyright laws and downloading is strictly prohibited. The right to reproduce or transfer the work via any medium must be secured with Farrar, Straus and Giroux.

Image Credits

62 (bl) looking up ©Carrie Garcia/HMH, skyline ©andersphoto/Shutterstock; (bc) ©Jean Marc-Giboux/HMH; 66 (t) ©Lester Laminack; (b) ©Heinemann; 68 (l to r) ©Radachynskyi Serhii/Shutterstock; ©Billion Photos/Shutterstock; ©Patrick Krabeepetcharat/Shutterstock; ©ChristianChan/Shutterstock; ©Alex006007/Shutterstock; ©ChristianChan/Shutterstock; ©Yakobchuk Vasyl/Shutterstock; ©Radachynskyi Serhii/Shutterstock; ©aslysun/Shutterstock; ©space_heater/Shutterstock; ©concept w/Shutterstock; ©Adriana/Adobe Stock; 120 ©Abigail Bobo/HMH; 126 Find Your Park: ©National Park Service, D.C